WITHDRAWN
WRIGHT STATE UNIVERSITY LIBRARIES

Now I Remember

Now I Remember:

Recovered Memories of Sexual Abuse

Charles R. Kelley, Ph.D.
Eric C. Kelley, B.A.

K/R Publications
Vancouver, Washington

Copyright © 1994 by Charles R. Kelley. All rights reserved. No part of this book may be used or reproduced in any manner without written permission of the copyright holder.

Book design and typography by John Laursen at Press-22.
Printed in the United States of America by Thomson-Shore, Inc.

ISBN 1-885643-00-4
Library of Congress Card Number 94-96158

K/R Publications
13717 Southeast 36th Street
Steamboat Landing
Vancouver, WA 98684-7770

Also by Charles R. Kelley

The Radix
A compilation, available in English and Spanish, of articles and monographs written between 1962 and 1992.
    Volume I: *Radix Personal Growth Work*
    Volume II: *The Science of Radix Processes*

Science and the Life Force
A correspondence course of nine monthly seminar and question-and-answer cassettes, with readings and assignments. Systematically explores the life force (radix) concept as the unifying bridge between mind and body, science and religion.

Contents

Preface ix

1 *Childhood Sexual Abuse and its Memory* 3

2 *The Nature of Memory* 14
Memory, Repression, and Traumatic Amnesia 15
Suggestion and Memory 18
Errors of Identification in Memory Recovery 19

3 *R-Memories and Psychotherapy* 25
Reflections on the Recovered Memory Therapy Movement 42

4 *R-Memories of Ritual Abuse and Alien Abduction* 45
Satanic Ritual Abuse (SRA) 46
Alien Abductions 51
Belief Systems and Pseudomemories of Sexual Abuse 52
Autism and Intermediaries 55

5 *Dealing with Memories of Incestuous Abuse* 59

   Continuous (Normal) Memories of Incestuous Abuse 60

   Dealing with Recovered Memories 68

   The Character of Those Having R-Memories 71

   Suggestions for Working with Clients
              Having R-Memories of Abuse 74

   How *Not* to Deal with R-Memories 78

   Treating Pseudomemories as Truth 82

6 *Commentary* 85

7 *Conclusion* 105

Glossary 108

Notes 111

References 117

Index 121

Preface

A generation ago, stories of sexual abuse committed against children within the family were unusual, and were met with skepticism. These abuse stories were often related by a victim to a disbelieving family member. The pain and alienation of a child who tells a trusted parent of such abuse and is met with skepticism or outright denial and accusations of lying are familiar to all helping professionals who have worked with abuse victims as adults. It compounds the devastation that sexual abuse itself wreaks on a victim's life. Our hearts go out to such victims, and much has been done by mental health professionals to help repair the damage done to them. Mental health professionals have learned to make it easier for other victims to come forward, to facilitate the disclosure of memories of abuse and work with the victim and, when appropriate, help in the taking of action against abusers.

Today, the situation has changed. In some places, disclosures still meet disbelief and denial, but much of society has awakened to the scope of the problem of child abuse. Some segments of society have overreacted, exaggerating the extent of the problem to the point where they see abuse when no abuse is present. Thus abuse has changed from being underreported to being overreported. It used to be that most reported child abusers were convicted. Now, despite a great increase in laws and funding, the

National Committee for Prevention of Child Abuse reports that only nineteen percent of reports of child abuse are substantiated.

Instances of sexual abuse have been widely publicized. Some of these are of recently discovered abuse of children; some are adults telling stories of long-remembered abuse. In recent years, many accusations of sex abuse have come from therapy clients who claim to have *recovered* memories of abuse in childhood years or decades after the fact, usually in the course of therapy designed to facilitate the process. As we shall see, such recovered memories can be true as remembered; they can be partially true, but garbled; and they can be objectively false, i.e., pseudomemories. Recovered memories are sometimes not memories at all, and we refer to them as *R-memories*, to distinguish them from ordinary, continuous memories. We include a small glossary of special terms, such as R-memories, near the end of this book, beginning on page 108.

R-memories concern memories or fantasies of painful or frightening events that may have happened and been pushed out of conscious awareness for years or decades. They can also be imagined into existence, disguised as a true memory, or they may be a mixture of truth and fantasy. They may appear spontaneously or through a process of therapy or personal growth. They typically occur in connection with therapy or self-help groups utilizing techniques such as hypnotic regression or waking suggestion. The client tends to lose contact with the immediate surroundings as powerful images from memory or fantasy or a mixture develop. This often involves development of a child-like state of mind in the client. The images may be horrendous, and experienced with a great deal of feeling. They may involve childhood sexual and physical abuse, and in some cases include scenes of forced participation in satanic religious rituals involving sexual acts, torture, and murder. Some therapists using hypnosis and regressive techniques evoke R-memories of abduction and sex abuse aboard alien space ships, or of traumas occurring in "past lives." The most frequent subject of R-memories, however, is childhood incestuous sexual abuse. Because of the extent and seriousness of child sex abuse, R-memories of abuse are a serious matter, both when they are true—reflecting actual criminal abuse—and when they are false or distorted and become the basis of untrue accusations against innocent parties.

Those having R-memories of abuse include celebrities and others who have made their stories public, writing books and appearing on television talk shows. Chicago's Cardinal Bernardin was accused of sodomizing a youth years after the alleged abuse, based on R-memories obtained through hypnosis. The charges, which appear to be baseless, were later withdrawn. Roseanne Barr Arnold has accused her father of sex abuse based on R-memories, which her parents and siblings vociferously deny ever happened. Lawsuits have been brought, sometimes successfully, by adults on the basis of R-memories of abuse in childhood. The accuser is typically a woman; the accused is her father, stepfather, grandfather, or older brother, sometimes her mother. Some alleged abusers have been jailed, one convicted of murder, solely on the evidence of R-memories of events that allegedly took place years ago but for which there was amnesia on the part of the victims or witnesses. Many of the accused claim innocence, and fault overeager therapists for convincing their children that they were abused. A father's lawsuit set a precedent in California when Gary Ramona sued his accusing daughter's therapists and a hospital. The jury awarded him $500,000 in damages. Some clients are suing their former therapists, accusing them of producing false R-memories that divided their family and otherwise disrupted their lives. Some individuals have retracted their accusations of abuse, saying they now recognize their R-memories were false. However, others accused on the basis of R-memories have admitted their guilt.

How are we to make sense of this issue? No one can say with certainty what proportions of R-memories are true, false, or garbled, but it is clear that false and garbled R-memories are common enough that no given R-memory can be fairly judged to be true without substantial evidence aside from the memory itself. The consequences of erroneously judging false R-memories to be true *or* true R-memories to be false can be severe, as we will see.

We published a series of articles on the subject of R-memories in 1993 in the *Chuck Kelley Radix Newsletter*. As our investigations progressed the subject caught fire in the press and on TV. Notables became involved, the media personalities, the Roman Catholic Cardinal. The situation surrounding recovered memories became more complex. New data appeared every few days, new cases, new findings to integrate. This book is the end result of our work. In it we have made use of material from our *Newsletter* articles, new information, and the comments and questions by readers of the *Newsletter* to forge a new, comprehensive treatment of the subject of recovered memories of sexual abuse. We will touch on the wider issues of child abuse, including the process of recovery from abuse, but the book is devoted to understanding R-memories, with primary attention to R-memories of incestuous childhood abuse that appear in adulthood. Numbers inserted in superscript refer to Notes, which follow the last chapter. They are comprised mostly of source information or of expansions of points made in the text.

A word needs to be said about the respective contributions of the authors. Charles, the senior author, wrote the three *Newsletter* articles the book was built around. The point of view in these articles has been maintained as the material grew into a book crafted by both of us. The original case histories and theory are by Charles and, whenever the text is in the first person singular, it is Charles speaking. Eric wrote the copy for most of Chapters One and Three and a few other sections; he reorganized and edited the *Newsletter* articles for the book, tackled the growing mountain of new material, and selected and wrote up most of the examples and cases taken from the literature that we have included. Charles

PREFACE

wrote most of the balance, with the examples from his own practice, the advice to those dealing with recovered memories (Chapter Five), and the dialog and response to commentary from readers of the *Newsletter* articles forming Chapter Six. We each critiqued and edited the other's material. Charles, as senior author, claims final word on the content.

Accounts from retractors who have recanted stories of abuse based on false memories have added an element to our work. Eleanor Goldstein and Kevin Farmer have gathered stories of retractors into a single volume, *True Stories of False Memories*, which we commend to readers. We thank the authors for giving us permission to quote freely from this volume. We also thank Pamela Freyd and her FMS Foundation, which contributed much useful information. See Notes, numbers two and three, for addresses.

We would like to thank some of those others who helped us in various ways. Erica Kelley's editing, design, and formatting skills contributed much to the final product, as they have to all the Kelley/Radix (K/R) publications through the years. Our *Newsletter* readers are an unusually informed and articulate group, as their commentary in Chapter Six shows. They have helped to round out our treatment, and we thank them each and all. And to those who have candidly shared their experiences and points of view in the literature contributing to this work, we express our appreciation.

Charles R. Kelley
Eric C. Kelley
April 1994

Now I Remember

1

Childhood Sexual Abuse and its Memory

Delving into issues surrounding the incestuous abuse of children brings up strong feelings in virtually everyone, for different reasons. Everyone was once a vulnerable, powerless child. Many were faced with physical or sexual abuse in their own families, or are close to people who went through a lot of pain from childhood abuse. The issue is loaded with feelings, so much so that facts are often confused or distorted. The problem is to find our way through the feelings and look with an uncompromising eye at the issue of recovered memories (R-memories) of abuse. The beginning point is abuse itself.

Incestuous sexual abuse of children is common. A *Los Angeles Times* phone survey found twenty-seven percent of women and sixteen percent of men had been sexually maltreated before the age of eighteen. Other sources give numbers ranging all the way from six percent to sixty-three percent.[1] Between twenty and twenty-five percent of the adult women on whom I have taken a sexual history have been victims of some kind of sexual abuse, and almost half the abuse was incestuous. Men I have interviewed have been sexually abused in childhood somewhat less than a third as often as women.

Incestuous sexual abuse, our concern, frequently causes lasting damage to the lives of its victims. And there are two classes of victims. The first is the abused, the child who has been victimized, second the adult who is falsely accused. Consider first the child. Here are a few examples from the senior author's sexual research experience:

Shirley, a woman of twenty-six, came from a broken home. Her father absent from early childhood, she lived with her mother and her maternal grandfather, a widower. The mother worked and was away from home much of the time, some of it for overnight stays with men friends. The mother was ungiving towards her only child, who was a burden to her, and was glad to see her own father become the primary care-giver. The little girl needed someone. The grandfather cared for her and loved her. He took her places, taught her to read, and so on. They were each the most important person in the other's life. And from the age of four, he abused her sexually.

She thought it started with him bathing her, washing and drying, and fondling her genital area. It soon developed into a bedtime pattern, however. He told her bedtime stories, fondling her body as he did so. He handled her everywhere, and played with her vagina and anus with his fingers. During the next years, he came to masturbate as he fondled her. She was sometimes encouraged to fondle his erect penis before he started his masturbatory movements, but he never tried to penetrate her and never ejaculated against her. He taught her she must never talk about "their secret."

It went on for more than five years. In school, Shirley became more and more uncomfortable about it. She told a trusted playmate, in confidence. Her friend told her it was awful, and if anyone found out, they'd take her grandfather away. That night she told her grandfather it was bad, and she didn't want it any more. Fortunately, he never tried again. — But she missed it, she said.

Shirley was deeply scarred by the incest experience, though it's hard to disentangle the effects of the abuse from the other stresses of her unhappy home. As an adult she felt wrong about her body and sexuality and, beyond that, about her basic self-worth, which caused her to seek professional help. She had learned to enjoy the grandfather's sexual fondling, and at the same time felt guilty and worthless. She tended to pull her awareness up into her head and out of her "bad" body. She didn't date in high school, though she was attractive enough and had offers. Her grandfather died when she was fifteen. She had sexual problems in marriage, but things were looking up with a new lover after the marriage broke up.

She refused to let the group she was in vilify her grandfather. "He gave me the only love I ever got," she said. "Maybe he was a dirty old man, but he took care of me, fed me, shopped for things with me, took me places. He made a life for me. Without him I would have had nothing!"

Incestuous child abuse is frequent and takes many forms, ranging from sexual fondling of the very young such as Shirley experienced to forcible rape and sodomy, the latter mostly with older children. Some incest is single occurrence, some repeated, sometimes over many years, as in the above example.

Here are other examples:

A woman client described being forcibly raped on several occasions by her fifteen-year-old brother. She was thirteen years old when it happened. He would do it when the parents were away. The parents steadfastly refused to believe her story. She thought the lack of support from her parents was as destructive as the rapes themselves.

Martha was brutally raped at the age of twelve by her stepfather, a one-time rape. How it was dealt with is told in Chapter Five.

A woman of thirty was abused as a young teenager by men picked up in bars by her mother, who were lured to her home by the promise of sex with her beautiful daughter. It is the mother's complicity that forms the incestuous element of this case. The daughter was thirteen the first time it happened. The woman described in moving detail how, when her mother brought another man home, she would stack the bed, her chest of drawers, everything against the door of her room, trying to wedge it shut. The men would always be able to force it open, and throw her down and rape her. There was one exception—when the man saw her he slapped the mother and said, "She's just a little kid! You ought to be ashamed."

At fifteen she met a sixteen-year-old prostitute who taught her how to live on the streets. She left home and never went back to it or saw her mother again. When she told her story she had two fatherless children but held a job, and had spent several years turning her life around, so the children wouldn't have to live as she had had to.

A forty-one-year-old man had lived with his mother all his life. In an individual sex research interview, he talked about his sex history. He described himself as having been a "mama's boy." He was shy, and he and his mother lived alone. He confided everything to her. Near puberty he told her about getting erections and having sexual tensions. She took it upon herself to teach him how to masturbate by doing it to him. The "lessons" became regular, two or three times per week, and had been continuing for nearly thirty years. He had only once had a brief, unsuccessful relationship with a woman his age, but his mother had "won him back," as she put it. He came in worried. His mother was getting older. . . .

> *A man of thirty-six related having been seduced by his sexually precocious fifteen-year-old niece. He was twenty-two at the time, and much less experienced than she. He was tempted to continue the relationship, but wisely stayed clear. She was legally a victim of incestuous child abuse and statutory rape, and he was a felon. The adult is responsible for exercising self-control in such cases.*

These are just a few of the many and varied cases which illustrate incestuous sexual abuse of a child. They all illustrate violation of the ancient taboo in its most taboo form, with a minor child in the abuser's family as the victim. Sexual abuse of children leaves deep and lasting scars in most cases. And there is one thing that all the above have in common. The victims remember them, and always have. They remember them vividly and describe them clearly.

Now consider the other kind of victim when there are accusations of incestuous child abuse today, that of those falsely accused of abuse as a result of R-memories. Again, an example:

> *Our case—On April 4th our daughter wrote to her father (seventy years old) and me (sixty-seven years old). She accused her father of molesting her over and over again and abusing her from ages three to eight. She accused her older brother of knowing about the abuse because, she said, his room was under the attic where it was supposed to have gone on. There was no attic in that house. I asked her to go with me to that house to see if there was an attic but she refused. On April 30th, my husband of forty-six years died of a ruptured aneurysm. I know he died of a broken heart.*
> *—A Mom*[2]

With stories like this the facts become shadowy. What actually happened in the woman's childhood? Was there an attic in that house? Was the daughter sexually abused by her father? Was she molested at another time or place, or by someone else? If the father was innocent, what happened to the daughter that produced her distorted or falsified memories? There are many of these kinds of cases in the literature, where abuse could not have happened as reported because (for example) the accused was out of the country when the alleged abuse occurred. Often other family members present in the house deny the possibility. In the overreaction of some people to the problem of incestuous child abuse, some people have made untrue accusations, typically as a result of R-memories. Frequently, it is not possible to know whether an R-memory with a resulting accusation is true or false.

Almost every author writing on the subject falls into one camp or the other on this issue of the truth or falsity of R-memories of abuse, and feelings run high on both sides. Some writers detail the destruction of families, undeserved punishment of the accused, and other harm done by false R-memories, and passionately denounce therapists for producing R-memories in clients that lead to false accusations. Others vigorously defend R-memory therapy, denouncing claims of "false memories" as systematic denial by abusers and their dupes, and as social backlash against the exposure of widespread incestuous child abuse.

A primary concern of this book is the accuracy of R-memories of sex abuse recovered after a long period. Many people today are questioning the authenticity of R-memories, at least of some R-memories. The movement to question them has developed around one organization in particular, the False Memory Syndrome Foundation (FMSF), based in Philadelphia but maintaining a network nationwide and abroad. Because of its pivotal role in the discussion, we will discuss and evaluate the FMSF here. The Foundation maintains that many therapists have encouraged or induced false R-memories in their clients, creating false histories of incestuous abuse, and have encouraged accusations of abuse against innocent people.

The work of the FMSF includes distributing publications by the many scientists that support the false memory concept, networking and keeping track of accused families, and publishing a monthly newsletter. These activities are supported primarily by parents accused by their grown children of childhood incestuous abuse on the basis of R-memories developed in connection with therapy or self-help groups. The Foundation also has a long and impressive list of academics—largely psychologists, both clinicians and researchers—who support their central thesis, that R-memories of abuse are often false. The *FMSF Newsletter* is filled with the stories of those claiming to be falsely charged. They detail the pain of such a charge from a loved child, the suffering from loss from their lives of children who cut off contact in the wake of a false R-memory. Grandchildren are often lost to their grandparents. Public denunciations, lawsuits and/or criminal charges may follow. Siblings of an accuser who have no memories of abuse occasionally develop R-memories of their own, or they believe the accuser and cut off the parents from their lives as well. But siblings usually contradict the allegations based on R-memories of a brother or sister, and their testimonials appear in the *FMSF Newsletter* and elsewhere.[3] The newsletter also gives information on relevant scientific work and updates on legal rulings.

In recent months, a new form of evidence and another kind of suffering related to this issue has been documented as large numbers of "retractors" have made their stories public. Retractors are people who have developed R-memories of incestuous abuse, made accusations based on them, and later concluded that their R-memories were false and retracted the accusations.[4] The FMS Foundation has heard from more than two hundred retractor families as of April 22, 1994. Retractors have organized among themselves, and published their own newsletter.[5] Retractors tell often horrendous stories of their experience in therapy. One woman describes her sister's condition when she recanted her accusations against the family:

> *She's a mess. She sounds terrible. She has nothing left, friends or money or job. Her insurance ran out and then she cashed in all her retirement money for therapy and then that ran out and she has not been in therapy. She owes money to the Internal Revenue Service. She wants to see Mom and Dad. She said that she loves them and that she doesn't believe in the horrible memories she had. What a waste!*[6]

Retractor testimony gives a new kind of credibility to the false memories position and provides insight into how false memories sometimes develop. A few retractors are now suing their former therapists, claiming the therapy produced false R-memories of childhood incest and encouraged them to act on them, severely disrupting the clients' lives and the lives of their families. Retractors, like accusers before them, have made talk show appearances describing their cases. The *FMSF Newsletter* has recently included more quotes from retractors and stories of reunions with accused parents. Testimonials by retractors figure prominently in our discussion of R-memories and psychotherapy in Chapter Three.

Many clinicians and some researchers criticize the false memory concept, taking issue with research cited to support the issue and branding it a way to further denial of sexual abuse. They point out that the FMS Foundation is founded and supported in large part by the accused, who have much to gain by discrediting their accusers. They accuse the Foundation of harboring abusers. They point to examples of corroborated recovered memories, and to siblings who develop R-memories after another child from the family has done so. The symptoms that usually exist before R-memories are recovered are also suggested as evidence for the authenticity of R-memories.

Supporters of the false memory concept cite the large amounts of money paid to R-memory therapists as motivation for creating R-memories—authentic or otherwise. A single client with R-memories of abuse can bring a therapist $100,000 or more in fees over the years. The costs can be much greater when clients are hospitalized. Both "sides" in the conflict about R-memories take issue with research reported and interpretations made that go against their position.

Because the "false memories" argument was largely initiated by and still revolves partly around the FMS Foundation, and because many who support the concept have ties to the FMSF, criticism of the false memory position sometimes takes the form of attacks on the credibility of the Foundation itself. While it is appropriate to discuss and evaluate the Foundation and its guiding members, the credibility of the organization and the truth or falsity of R-memories are separate issues.

The False Memories Syndrome Foundation was founded in March of 1992 by Drs. Pamela and Peter Freyd, a married academic couple, in the wake of their elder daughter Jennifer's R-memories and subsequent accusation that Peter sexually abused her as a child. Pamela Freyd is the executive director of the Foundation. In 1991 she published a description of her perspective on her daughter's accusations, writing under the pseudonym "Jane Doe."[7] In this article she denied that there was any possibility that her daughter's R-memories of abuse could have taken place as described. Their daughter revealed herself and commented on her situation in August of 1993 in a public address.[8] Jennifer Freyd, a college professor and Ph.D. psychologist herself, defends the truth of her R-memories, in which she came to remember experiences of her father molesting her during most of her childhood, beginning at age three or four, raping her when she was sixteen. She claimed that she had lost all memory of this repeated childhood sexual abuse until she recovered her memories at thirty-three in therapy. She also accuses her father of alcoholism and of sexual innuendoes made to her in her childhood and adulthood which she says she remembers apart from her R-memories.

Her parents claim her R-memories are false and were induced by her therapy. They allege that her therapist began delving after sexual abuse in the second session, and assigned the book *The Courage to Heal: A Guide for Women Survivors of Child Sexual Abuse*[9] in the third. They quote her therapist as saying that she diagnoses incest or sexual abuse in seventy to eighty percent of her clients. *The Courage to Heal* has been denounced by critics as an instruction manual for producing false memories of abuse.

This family tragedy illustrates the human side of the recovered memories dispute. Jennifer has cut off contact with her parents. If her R-memories are true, who can blame her? And if her R-memories are false, a family has been destroyed by pseudomemories created by her therapy two decades after her imaginary abuse. Readers wishing further details on this case may read what is published for themselves.[10] But whether Jennifer's R-memories are true or false, the issues concerning the truth or falsity of R-memories go far beyond any one case or organization.

Critics dismiss the FMS Foundation as a tool of abusers who are collecting arguments to further their own denial of the abuse they perpetrate or have perpetrated. One clinician wrote: "In our perpetrators' program, many individuals who had previously acknowledged their perpetrations have begun carrying around 'false memory' articles to fuel their denial, resulting in more perpetrations."[11] It's not clear how carrying the articles was supposed to have produced "more perpetrations," i.e., more acts of abuse.

It is likely that some abusers are drawn to and hide behind false memory arguments. However, it is far-fetched to brand all the work of the Foundation and of independent scientists pointing out that R-memories are often untrue as existing to further the denial of parents that they incestuously abused their children. That is equivalent to saying all therapists dealing with R-memories are running a money-making racket that is based on producing false memories in their clients.

Parents accused of abuse based on R-memories are sometimes allowed by therapists to see their children only on the condition that they "acknowledge their perpetrations"—a possible motive for acknowledging abuse that didn't happen. Perhaps their children's therapists told them, as others have been told, that their children were suicidal and would take their own lives if their memories were not confirmed![12] False memory articles no doubt fuel denial by some incestuous abusers—just as support by therapists of false R-memories fuels false accusations of serious criminal acts against innocent people.

We will begin our effort to better understand R-memories by considering the nature of human memory itself.

2
The Nature of Memory

The starting point for understanding R-memories is the nature of memory itself. Memory is *not* a process of recording our experiences, which can then be accessed and replayed. Traces of past sights, sounds, etc. provide us with pieces and fragments of a past experience which we assemble at the moment of recall into a framework we provide that gives the pieces and fragments meaning. The memory we put together is not a replaying of a recording, but a creation in our mind in the present of an image, story, etc. of a past event, the cues for which are partial and incomplete. I.M.L. Hunter wrote in his book on memory:

> Our account of an event is usually not so much an accurate reproduction as an elaboration of fragmentary recollections into a coherent caricature of the original. In the light of our general expectations about events, we construct, out of a few elements, an account of what was likely to have occurred.[13]

As a consequence, different people recalling the same event are likely to remember it very differently. Court witnesses to an accident or crime who are honest and telling the truth as they remember it tell strikingly dissimilar and even contradictory recollections of the same event. Psychologists have staged unexpected dramas in front of classes of students, all of whom later wrote accounts or completed questionnaires about what happened in the drama. The accounts are amazingly different.[14]

It is normal in remembering for memories to "fill in" as they are described, and for some details to be recovered. The filling-in of detail involves a combination of recollection and imagination, as the rememberer strives to create a consistent story of what happened from the fragments and traces of the past that memory supplies. The imagined details take their place in the constructed memory side by side with the remembered events. The process of filling gaps in memory by imagination is called *confabulation*. Confabulation should not be confused with lying. We are usually unaware that our confabulations are products of our imagination. As the memory process develops, the recovered and the confabulated details are integrated to form the memory. Normal memories are made up of the truly remembered and the gaps "filled in" by confabulation. The gaps occur because all memory is partial and incomplete. Such gaps in normal memory are *not* created by repression of painful, frightening, or otherwise upsetting material. If the memory involved is a painful one, the central, painful facts—things which most capture the attention—are what are remembered. The context in which the facts are imbedded, what happened before, around, and after the trauma, contains the gaps filled in during recollection.

Memory, Repression, and Traumatic Amnesia

In authentic R-memories, gaps in memory are created by a different process entirely. Here, the gaps involve the central elements of the memory, not the peripheral context. They are not a consequence of normal forgetting of the less important material, but the blocking out of that which is most important because remembering it is in some degree unpleasant or distressing. In Freudian parlance, the blocked material is *repressed*. The key feature of repressed material is that the unavailability of the selected material to memory is temporary and reversible. The concept is best applied to such things as blocking on the memory of a name, forgetting an appointment, misplacing an object one is using, for psychological reasons. These can be discovered through free association. Freud wrote a great deal about the process.[15]

The concept of Freudian repression as applied to memories of abuse is not accepted by all psychologists.[16] Experimental psychologists are not in agreement that repression and derepression (remembering formerly repressed material) exist in the form that most incest recovery therapists assume, much less that they play the role in the memory of traumatic abuse claimed by large numbers of clinicians. In my own professional experience, Freudian repression and derepression is almost universal, while full-fledged *amnesia* for traumatic past events is rare. People seldom forget automobile accidents, robberies and muggings, or their house burning down, nor do they normally forget being raped or sodomized. Yet in rare cases there *is* amnesia for major traumatic events. Some soldiers shell-shocked in combat "forget" scenes of horror and stress beyond their ability to cope. Unbearable stress at home may produce a "fugue" that involves flight to another city or town with amnesia for the past and, after recovery, amnesia for the fugue period. And in some minority of cases of incest, there is traumatic amnesia for the experience.

Both the concept of repression and the discovery of R-memories should be credited to Freud. In the formative early years of psychoanalysis, Freud used both hypnosis and free association in tracing back the history of the symptoms of hysteric patients.[17] In so doing he ran into an obstacle that he said was almost fatal to psychoanalysis:

> Under the influence of the theory of traumatic hysteria, following Charcot, one was easily inclined to regard as real and as of etiological importance the accounts of patients who traced back their symptoms to passive sexual occurrences in the first years of childhood—speaking frankly, to seductions. When this etiology broke down through its own unlikelihood, and through the contradiction of well-established circumstances, there followed a period of absolute helplessness. The analysis had led by the correct path to such infantile sexual traumas, and yet, these were not true. Thus, the basis of reality had been lost. . . . If hysterics trace back their symptoms to imaginary traumas, then this new fact signifies that they create such scenes in phantasy, and hence psychic reality has to be given a place next to actual reality.[18]

Thus in regressive therapy with hysteric patients, Freud's patients regressed further and further, recovering memories of incest in early childhood. Investigation showed these R-memories could not be true; they were pseudomemories. By recognizing them as pseudomemories, Freud was able to analyze further, to understand how the pseudomemories were fantasies covering autoerotic activities of the child, after which, he said, the whole sexual life of the child came to light. The discovery of pseudomemories of incest thus led Freud to his understanding of infantile sexuality, which became the cornerstone of psychoanalytic theory. The sexuality of early childhood, where fact merges with fantasies, plays a special role in the field of sex abuse and memories of sex abuse.

Nearly a century later Jeffrey Masson, a psychoanalyst and one-time director of Freud's archives, tried to resurrect Freud's abandoned early view that the many R-memories of incest by hysteric patients in psychoanalysis were real.[19] The corollaries to this suggestion are: first, that father-daughter incest was far more common than anyone had believed in Freud's time; and second, that it played an important role in the etiology of hysteria. The first corollary is no doubt true. The second, however, is extremely dubious. Freud buckled to pressure, Masson claimed. Radical feminists seized on Masson's suggestion, and it was widely discussed.

In our opinion, Masson is neither a good theoretician nor a wise clinician, and his suggested revision of Freud is not the product of scholarship and sound clinical research but of an ambitious man riding the politics of his profession. Radical feminists, who are quick to attack Freud and/or fathers, rallied to his viewpoint. But a serious question such as the origin of hysteria cannot be decided on the basis of ideology or political agenda. The basic character structure Freud called the hysteric is set early in the child's life, well before most incest takes place. People with every character structure, not just Freud's hysterics, are sometimes victims of incest and other child abuse. Hysteria and suggestibility go hand-in-hand, and it appears likely that the same process was at work with Freud and the incest memories of his patients as is today producing pseudomemories in the recovered memory therapy movement. The hysteric character structure Freud most often worked with has played a large role in both, a role in need of further investigation. The term "hysteric" has come into some disfavor in the past thirty years because it is sometimes used in a manner deprecating to women. We discuss it further in Chapter Five and in the Glossary.

Suggestion and Memory

Memories can be modified and falsified with relative ease by hypnotic techniques and by waking suggestion. Elizabeth Loftus, a researcher specializing in memory at the University of Washington, describes suggestive techniques by means of which false memories were implanted in experimental subjects. A fourteen-year-old subject listened to a fictitious story of a time when he, as a small child, was lost in a shopping mall. The story was told as if true by the subject's older brother. The subject developed a detailed memory of the "event," reporting it just as the brother had described, with elaborations and with firm conviction in the reality of the event.[20] Loftus cites other examples. The form of suggestion influencing memory that we are most concerned with is the suggestion of incest in the books, groups, and the direct process of memory recovery therapy. Some therapists suggest strongly that patients having no memory of incest were, in fact, incest victims. Others suggest patients were victims of satanic ritual abuse. In each case, the driving force underlying the suggestibility is a potent belief system, usually backed by an individual who is accepted as an authority, i.e. the therapist.

Again, we must take stock. It would be a grave mistake to assume that all R-memories of abuse are false. Sexual abuse is appallingly common and, even though amnesia is rare, there is sometimes amnesia for traumatic events. When we meet with an R-memory of abuse, we cannot be sure on the face of it if the memory is true, false, or partially true and partially false, as when there are errors of identification of principal characters in the memories.

Errors of Identification in Memory Recovery

Repression and amnesia take an event out of the normal process of memory into the underground of unconscious processes. When the event emerges as R-memory, it may have undergone more transformation and distortion than is typically the case with ordinary memory. For instance, abuse may be remembered, but the abuser misidentified. A forty-year-old man recovered, through regressive therapy, the R-memory of his grandfather molesting him sexually as a small child. Family members were most upset at the allegation. Details of the story were later reported to the man's uncle, son of the accused grandfather, who said, "No, that was not Dad, that was me." The uncle went on to relate how, as a teenager experimenting sexually, he had molested his young nephew just as the nephew came to remember in his therapy but had blamed on the innocent grandfather.[21]

Another example of misidentification came to us from a former student, Jay Rubin, a neo-Reichian teacher and a reader of our *Newsletter*. The story shows some of the dynamics of false memory formation. He called it "A Case of 'Incestuous Sexual Abuse'":

Laurel (a pseudonym) and I were best friends from the dawning of my memory. We played in all the ways children will. Occasionally she would suggest a game she called "turkey." She was the turkey and I was the "buyer." She would lay naked on her back with her arms and legs folded up like a dressed turkey. It was my job to gently squeeze ("chubbing" her was what she called it) every part of her body (certain areas more thoroughly than others) to determine whether or not she had reached the optimum plumpness. I was to insert my finger into her various orifices to make sure she was clean and "hollow" and "ready for the stuffing." If not yet plump-enough, she would eat another candy bar. When finally plump-enough, a minute or two of "cooking" (tense silence) was observed, after which I was to untie her "wings" and "drumsticks," pry her thighs apart to see if they separated easily from the hips (a test of "doneness"), and finally "carve her" at the joints with wooden popsicle sticks and slowly slobber and munch whatever part she thought should be "eaten." She would take the occasional "taste" of herself. Sometimes one of us would have to visit the kitchen for some salad dressing to vary the flavor. "Hmm. . . ," "pretty scrumptious."

Occasionally, I was the turkey, but she deemed me "too tough" to really be good in the role of a juicy turkey. In any case, she was softer and more "turkeyish" so she usually insisted on being in the role of turkey, which was fine with me. Neither of us fully understood exactly what we were doing but we both knew the game was totally absorbing. Riveting. Fascinating.

At the end of fifth grade her father was given a three-year appointment in Europe. I didn't see her again for forty years.

Last spring we were both at the wedding of a mutual friend's daughter and got to talking about our lives in the intervening years. She shared that she had been in alcohol recovery and in therapy. Among her therapeutic issues was the matter of her "sexual abuse" at the hands of her oldest brother. After maybe an hour of gently questioning her about the abuse, she shared that he had forced her to play this weird "sicko" game called "turkey" and that the abuse had gone on for a number of years. Memories of it had caused her years of nightmares and bizarre feelings in her body. She drank, she said, to quell anxiety provoked by these feelings. She told me that sex with her husband brought up the memories so strongly that it had nearly ended her marriage. Her brother (who "is in denial about it," she says) had, coincidentally, stopped making her play the game at around the same time that the family moved to Europe (away from me).

The setting of our conversation, the wedding reception, seemed an inappropriate time for me to inject my own memories. I intend to tell her about my memories, and to share with her the similar problems that I have had to work through, over the years, as a result of having experienced such strong, whole-body, sexual feelings before I was physically able to discharge them orgastically. Those games of "turkey" were among the most significant events in my own emotional life.

We wrote back to Mr. Rubin, and he wrote an "update" to the case which appears in Chapter Three (page 28). We can see the distorted view "Laurel" came to take of her memories. Of course, we cannot be sure if or to what degree our writer's memories are accurate. It appears that Laurel's brother is innocent of sexually abusing her, and she has distorted the memory of an intense, often repeated sex game with a playmate into a memory of incestuous abuse by her older brother, perhaps under the influence of a therapist's ideology.

Errors of identification are frequent with recovered memories. A student of mine developed an R-memory of sexual abuse she suffered as a young child at the hands of her grandfather. Over time she remained confident that she had been abused as she remembered, but was no longer sure that it was her grandfather who had been her abuser. Nothing had been done to lead her to doubt the R-memory or the identity of the remembered abuser.

Another example of "misidentification" betrays the accuser's state of mind. Paul McHugh, Professor and Director of the Department of Psychiatry at Johns Hopkins University School of Medicine, writes:

> A woman called her mother to claim that she had come to realize that when she was young she was severely and repeatedly sexually molested by her uncle, the mother's brother. The mother questioned the daughter carefully about the dates and times of these incidents and then set about determining whether they were in fact possible. She soon discovered that her brother was on military service in Korea at the time of the alleged abuse. With this information, the mother went to her daughter. . . . [T]he daughter seemed momentarily taken aback, but then said, "I see, Mother. Yes. Well, let me think. If your dates are right, I suppose it must have been Dad."[22]

What looks like misidentification could be someone shifting blame to another to prevent their pseudomemory from being disproven.

And it's possible that this woman was abused, but didn't know who the abuser was and was simply too quick to point fingers.

So R-memories of abuse may misidentify the abuser, and may be false in other ways. There may be a plastic, uncertain quality of the memories. The facts become cloudy and difficult or impossible to determine. Such R-memories, extracted as they are from the pool of the unconscious, may contain distortions or confabulations as to what happened, if it really happened, and when, where, and with whom it happened. Professor John F. Kihlstrom, Editor of *Psychological Science*, the journal of the American Psychological Society, is a psychologist of impeccable credentials. He has written of R-memories as follows:

> Near the beginning of their chapter on "Remembering," Bass and Davis write: "There is no right or wrong when it comes to remembering." Unfortunately, that's not remotely true. Memories are personal, and nobody can say to someone else that they don't have a particular memory. And, for that matter, nobody can say to someone else that they do have a particular memory, but they just can't remember it. But that doesn't mean that there is no right or wrong in memory. The crucible for memory is the truth about what happened, the fact of the matter. Incest and other forms of abuse and trauma occur all too frequently in our society, and the survivors of these experiences deserve our respect and support. But uncorroborated memories of these sorts of things have no special status. They should be taken seriously, and they should be investigated, but they should not be accepted uncritically by either the patient who remembers them or the therapist who receives the report. There is a fact of the matter, and the truth sometimes lies elsewhere.[23]

Well said, Dr. Kihlstrom! Yes, there is indeed a fact of the matter, and we should not confuse the fact with the memory, with its possibilities for error or distortion.

In the pages that follow we quote stories from retractors, therapy patients who come to believe their R-memories are false. Retractor stories are often dramatic and are becoming more and more widespread.[24] They leave little doubt that false memories are often created in therapy situations. Where do false R-memories "come from?" How could someone have a powerful, vivid memory of a trauma that never took place?

3
R-Memories and Psychotherapy

Certain psychotherapists employ special techniques designed to bring hidden memories of abuse into conscious awareness. Unfortunately, as we have seen, the "memories" that emerge can be inaccurate in important ways or can be entirely false, i.e. pseudo-memories. Some practitioners know this and are careful about how they apply these techniques, making sure they lead their clients as little as possible and watching themselves for inappropriate suggestions. On the other hand, others believe in, dredge for, and encourage their clients to act on R-memories when there is no real evidence of their genuineness. Here is a quotation from a popular book on sex abuse by Renee Fredrickson:

> Let yourself know what the most hopeless or shameful problem in your life is. Try saying to yourself three or four times a day for one week, "I believe this problem is about my repressed memories of abuse." After a week, write down or talk over with a friend how you see the problem now. Speculate on how it may relate to how you were abused.[25]

A person looking for the cause of a grave personal problem is thus encouraged to find or fabricate an abuse history that may or may not be accurate. This kind of suggestion is one reason why some therapists are justifiably accused of manufacturing false memories of abuse.

But can this kind of technique or any other really produce a false memory? Retractor testimony indicates that it can. The following comes from a woman who became very depressed after difficult circumstances in her life. She had considerable abuse in her history that she had always remembered. She developed a dependence on her therapist, who became convinced that her patient had been a victim of satanic ritual abuse and repressed the memory. She had been pressured to "remember" before she came to this session, and had been having nightmares.

> *One morning, after a night filled with nightmares, Dr. D___ took me into a room to have what I thought was going to be a "Hi, how are you today?" visit. This particular day she insisted that I confront my bad dreams head on. The only problem was that we were not talking about my nightmares. She told me to close my eyes and relax. She started describing a cold dark place and asked me what I could see in my mind's eye. I said I saw a large slab of stone. She said, "Like an altar?" I was to continue to look closer and tell her who was there. In my imagination I remember feeling child-like and peeking out of a corner. The doctor then described a baby to me which I saw as a woman giving birth. We then continued as she asked me questions about people in black hooded robes and magically, when she said things, I saw them. She asked about candles. I [sic] talked about daggers and oh yes, I saw those too. She asked me to describe the setting again, and I began to ramble on about the woman giving birth. I know that at some point I asked her to stop. She sounded a bit frustrated, but insisted we continue. Her voice sounded calmer now as she spoke about the hooded people, the setting and the baby. So we looked into this movie as we put it together in my mind. She asked more about the woman*

giving birth. As we continued, I saw the baby coming out, covered in blood, and then came the afterbirth. It looked pretty gross. I felt frightened. When I had given birth to my second child, not all the afterbirth came out, and I passed it the next day. I felt panicky, like when it had happened to me in real life. Dr. D__ asked me what they were doing to the baby. All I could see was them taking the baby away. It was so strange. When she asked me how many people were there, all I could say was I didn't know, because as I looked at this mind image, one minute there would be three and the next about fifteen. She asked me again about the baby and suddenly my heart began to beat faster as I saw some beings, half human and half moles (mole people, I guess) and they were eating the afterbirth. I screamed out, "They're eating the afterbirth!" Next she asked me what I was doing. I kept saying, "I don't know." Then she surprised me by asking, "Are you eating the afterbirth too?" Suddenly in my mind <u>I was!</u> I started screaming hysterically. The doctor shouted for staff and medication. They made me chew a pill as I sobbed, clung to people, and hysterically relived what I at that time had believed to be a memory. Dr. D__ left sometime during this. I don't remember her saying goodbye.[26]

Thus an R-memory of satanic ritual abuse was created. Other retractors report using self-hypnosis, dream work, and other similar techniques under their therapists' guidance to try to "find memories." Another example:

I began having dreams of being raped. . . . Ann [her therapist] told me the dreams were symbolic of the repressed memories of incest in my subconscious mind. This was a good sign in my healing. She encouraged me to concentrate on my repressed memories and other problems right before falling asleep. She said my subconscious mind would work on them while I slept. She directed me to keep a notebook and pen at my bedside to record my dreams, saying they would reveal details to me about my molestation and my denial. While still groggy in the morning after first waking, I was to do self-hypnosis. She said that was a good time to try to access my subconscious mind.

Whereas I had done self-hypnosis once in a while in therapy with Tom, in my current desperation, I was now doing it once a day. I was taught that everything that had ever happened to me was on file in my mind. Now, daily, I would talk to my mind like it was a computer, saying pull up such and such a file.[27]

In addition to the possibility of developing false memories, the nature of memory is such that actual experiences are often later remembered very differently from the original event. Here also, the influence of therapist suggestion and regressive techniques can play a role. The following is an update to the case of "Laurel," a childhood playmate of correspondent Jay Rubin. Laurel came to remember their childhood sex game of "turkey" as incestuous abuse by her older brother, as presented in Chapter One. Our correspondent continues the story:

Some months later, I decided to set the record straight and to try to collect more information for this submission, and called Laurel for the first time ever. She sounded anxious and a bit hostile when I brought up her sexual abuse, but answered my questions. I first asked whether the rest of her family had been made aware of the older brother's misdeeds. The answer was "<u>Of course!</u> You didn't think that I would <u>protect</u> him, did you?!" I asked if she had told the family about the incidents as they were happening or shortly thereafter. "Are you kidding? You knew my parents. . . . They wouldn't have believed me. They were so 'proper.'" I asked when it was that she finally did tell them. "After I remembered it in therapy. . . about eight years ago. I guess I couldn't stand to remember who it was until it was fi-

nally brought out in a safe situation. . . a lot of people don't remember stuff like that, you know." I asked her if she had absolutely no recollection of it until it was "recovered" in therapy. She said that she had had dreams over the years involving a (faceless) "man" playing with her. The dreams had always been pleasurable, she said, but they frightened her upon awakening and thinking about them. "It just felt so wrong. . . and especially after I realized that the 'man' was my brother."

I understood this to mean that she had always been <u>vaguely</u> aware of having played the game, but that the (mis)identification of her brother and her determining the game to be abuse had developed during the course of "therapeutic" dredging, and that her real discomfort was rooted not so much in the nature of the game or feelings she had while playing the game, but rather, in feelings and thoughts surrounding the erroneous notion (memory) that her brother had been the other player.

I finally told her about <u>my</u> memories of playing the game with her, often at her suggestion, for hours at a time, and of my mother's memory of "breaking us up" and sending her home after catching us at that game a couple of times. I asked her as gently as I could if there is any chance that she came to remember what we did as something her brother did to her. I felt certain that this revelation of myself as "abuser" would lead to an instant "correction" of her memory, an "aha" experience. It did not. The suggestion was met with too-angry denial and the conversation quickly devolved into anxious silence and sarcasm—"You only wish" and other defensive attitudes. I ended by asking her to at least give the possibility some thought, and reminded her of the pet name by which she often, laughingly, called my penis during those games. I'm sure she <u>will</u> think about it, but her having already exposed her brother as an "incestuous pervert" to the family and others may well make her acceptance of my proposed correction very emotionally, and *practically, difficult. My hope is that she is now, or will become, big enough emotionally, and honest enough intellectually, to take the leap. I have no idea when, or if, I will hear from her again.*

We agree with our writer's interpretation that events which did not constitute abuse were reinterpreted and construed as abuse, probably under therapist influence.

According to the literature of the incest recovery movement, a wide range of symptoms can be attributed to past abuse that may or may not be remembered. *The Courage to Heal,* by Ellen Bass and Laura Davis, has been called the Bible of incest memory recovery therapy, with more than half a million copies sold.[28] This book comes up again and again in the stories of retractors and the accused. The book lists seventy-four questions in its "Taking Stock" section, and implies that some answers indicate a history of sexual abuse. Some questions clearly would denote incest, but others are much more ambiguous. Some examples:

Do you feel different from other people? (p. 35)

Do you have trouble expressing your feelings? (p. 35)

Do you ever use alcohol, drugs, or food in a way that concerns you? (p. 36)

Are you able to stay present when making love? (p. 37)

Shortly before this, readers were told:

If you think you were abused and your life shows the symptoms, then you were. (p. 22)

And later:

Many women don't have memories, and some never get memories. This doesn't mean they weren't abused. (p. 81)

Thus, virtually any symptoms of unhappiness or dysfunction—feeling different from others, inappropriate use of alcohol, trouble expressing feelings—are said to be indicative of a history of abuse, whether or not memories of abuse are present. Anyone who has such "symptoms" and can be made to think they were abused is in effect told by these "experts" that they *were* abused.

Another retractor's story brings us the extreme of creative interpretation of symptoms. She writes of the treatment she received in a psychiatric hospital:

> *Everything was interpreted as supporting the abuse. . . . Another technique they used was called "body memories." They believed that certain physical sensations reflected abuse that couldn't be remembered. That is, although there were no conscious memories, the body remembered. They told me that because I had some numbness in my hand, it was a result of holding my father's penis. Actually, the reason I had numbness in my hand was from taking 900 milligrams of Lithium and a large dose of Xanax and Mellaril. This made my fingers numb. My feeling of discomfort did not mean I wanted to cut off my hand because I'd touched my dad's penis. But that is what I was told it meant.*[29]

Some symptoms are caused, not by abuse, but by a belief in false memories of abuse! An example:

> *I know that during the time that I had false memories, my depression was probably not only due to my belief that I had been so violently betrayed by a trusted parent, but also due to the conflict I constantly experienced. (I was always thinking, "Could this really have happened to me?") When I resolved the inner conflict by making a final decision as to which memories were false, I was no longer depressed and no longer needed anti-depressants to cope.*[30]

Most people who go to a therapist are in distress—depressed, troubled about feelings they have and/or events in their lives. Therapists carry the same mantle of authority as doctors or other "experts" in many people's minds. This makes many clients vulnerable to suggestion and eager to please the therapist, whom they look to for the answer to their problems. In this delicate situation, there is direct and indirect suggestion of childhood abuse, even in the first session or initial interview. Documented examples of statements made by therapists include:

> Your symptoms sound like you have been abused when you were a child. What can you tell me about that? . . .
>
> You sound like the sort of person who must have been sexually abused. Tell me what that bastard did to you.[31]
>
> [After three months of therapy] I know everything about you and, anywhere between the ages of four and six, you were sexually abused as a child by your father.[32]

One woman with ten years' work experience in mental health wrote about her first session with a therapist:

> *What an amazing experience! After 1½ hours he told me I had MPD* [Multiple Personality Disorder]. *Even one of my alternate personalities came out while he was talking to me and my parents were Satan worshippers and I had been gang raped by the cult. When I refuted this he told me I was in denial and would not be whole again until I remembered all these things and worked through them. He also said that was the reason I was so overweight.*[33]

Hospitalized patients find themselves immersed in the ideology of the hospital staff day in and day out. Several retractors have written about daily intensive psychotherapy aimed at "recovering memories." Said one such writer, upon entering a psychiatric hospital for treatment for depression:

> *Right away I was met with questions about my parents. . . . My therapist asked me several times if I had ever been touched in a sexual manner. I replied, "No, not that I remember." He placed great emphasis on this possibility, as though I were withholding something very important that would explain my emotional problems. I started to think, "Well, if he thinks this is so important, maybe it is."* [34]

To the extremists, it is not enough if a client remembers neglect or emotional abuse or even some sexual abuse. Strong symptoms, it is believed, must imply incest and memory repression. One retractor had continuous memories of being physically abused by her mother and of watching her alcoholic father beat her mother. Her therapist insisted that she must have been sexually molested by her father:

> *Time and again I questioned Ann* [her therapist] *as to whether my symptoms couldn't be related to the traumas I remembered from childhood. Time and time again she firmly rebuked me with the pet phrase, "Trust me! It happened!"* [35]

Another retractor says of the beginning of her involvement with recovered memory therapy:

> *Yes, I was sexually abused by my uncle. . . . I always remembered this abuse and the exact details. I told my therapist about this abuse over the phone in our initial conversation. Then in the first day of group we discussed this and he said that he thought something else must have happened to me because I could talk about the abuse by my uncle too easily. He began to insinuate, and then to right-out say my parents must have known. He kept asking why wouldn't they rescue little Jennifer. Everyone was "on the hunt" for abuse.*

> *The memories of abuse by my uncle never changed during therapy, but I developed new "memories" of abuse by my father. My therapist even began to convince me that my dad probably wasn't even my biological dad and this would explain why he would abuse me.*[36]

In a similar vein, recovered memory therapists have shown a sometimes strong inclination to ignore current life problems to dredge for childhood memories of incest. Thus important, immediate personal problems can go untreated by the therapy and get worse. Indeed, dredging for memories has, for some retractors, absorbed time and energy that could otherwise have been used to work on the problems that led them to seek therapy in the first place! A retractor with lifelong emotional problems sought therapy after giving birth to a daughter with a rare life-threatening brain disease:

> *Although I could easily explain my desperate situation, my therapists insisted that all of my problems were based on my childhood. I received little or no help in dealing with the life-threatening illness of my baby, my marital problems, or the unresolved breakup of my first marriage. . . .*
>
> *I was able to relate several stories about inappropriate behavior from other adults of my childhood, true memories about being raped by a friend's brother, and sexual harassment as a teen by older men. Even so he* [her therapist] *seemed more interested in pulling out stories about my parents.*
>
> *As our relationship grew he was able to convince me that I must find the "truth" and work through it. He said this was the only way I could learn to overcome my anxiety. I thought I must be wrong for experiencing so much fear at the thought of my daughter's possible death because all my therapists seemed concerned about was my childhood.*[37]

Alongside suggestion and "expert" opinion, social groups often contribute greatly to the pressure to have "memories." When we first began our research into this topic it seemed that most false memories came from highly suggestible people who developed pseudomemories rather easily in regressive therapy, then came to believe in them and act accordingly. Reading retractors' stories paints a different picture in the majority of cases. The suggestive techniques are surely important, but of overriding importance for many retractors is the unrelenting pressure from the "new family" of their therapy group and from their therapists to "get their memories." This pressure they might feel for months or years without having clear "recollections" of abuse. Clients often become highly dependent on the social framework surrounding their therapy. In this context of dependence and pressure, clients and patients: are hypnotized and use self-hypnosis or other suggestive techniques to find memories; are told to believe their nightmares as memories; are told they're in denial, implying weakness, if they can't find (read "or fabricate") memories. This pervasive, persistent pressure, combined with their growing dependence, makes them vulnerable to the influence of these techniques.

Once R-memories develop, doubts about their authenticity often also appear. Such doubts are likely to be dismissed as denial by those attached to working with memories. A retractor writes of her therapy group:

> *If someone had some doubt that a flashback or memory was reality, Steve and Dave* [the therapists and group leaders] *would goad them, then the whole group would join in—"you're in denial," "you want to stay sick for your family," "you don't want to get well." This type of input from people we trusted so very much kept us enmeshed in their treatment program.*[38]

Other quotes:

> *I kept telling the therapist that I felt like I was making it all up and yet he assured me that people don't make up horrible experiences like that.*[39]

> *It has been our experience that the "recovered memories" that we believed for a time to be real were visualizations that our therapists encouraged. . . . If a therapist's role is to "validate" a person's deepest feelings, then what went wrong here when we said that we felt like we were making it up? . . . When we questioned, we were told that we were in denial or that the memories didn't feel real because we "hadn't owned or processed them yet."*[40]

Being abused and in denial means that one needs intensive therapy. And being unable to produce memories is simply a sign of denial, an indication that further therapy is needed. Such is the logic offered by recovered memory therapists. A retractor writes:

> *I wanted it over with once and for all! I decided I had to get back into individual therapy—I had only been attending group—and once and for all stop denying. I was desperate.*
>
> *Determined to come out of denial, I began hypnotherapy again.*[41]

R-memories will likely appear. And R-memories in themselves are widely regarded as all the proof needed to know for sure that one was abused as remembered. Hard evidence is not necessary. In *The Courage to Heal*, Bass and Davis imply that the story should be believed entirely on one's word. A letter to Laura Davis from a family member stated that rape and incest were heinous crimes, and called for factual evidence. This was the published response:

> Of course, such demands for proof are unreasonable. You are not responsible for proving that you were abused. (p. 137)

As a result, those accused of abuse are required to prove a negative: "prove it never happened." This is usually impossible, especially when the abuse allegedly occurred years or decades ago. It reverses the normal concept of justice. Someone accused of incestuous abuse is considered guilty if they don't prove themselves innocent!

When R-memories appear, R-memory therapists often encourage or mandate cutting off contact with anyone who does not believe in the R-memories, ostensibly to create safety for the recovery process. For a "survivor" who is involved in R-memories of abuse, a friend or family member who does not fully believe in the R-memories as truth is "in denial," and is failing to accept the rememberer's pain. Such a person is dangerous to the healing process and must be cut out of the "survivor's" life. Thus clients in therapy are isolated from other interpretations that could lead them to question their memories, and from the well-established fact that R-memories can be false.

> *All friends and family who didn't go along with our "diagnosis"* [of Multiple Personality Disorder] *were to be avoided, cut out of our lives, or considered perpetrators.*[42]

> *Tom and Ann* [her therapists] *had taught me that anyone who questions the validity of my repressed memories is denying my pain and doesn't really care about me. . . .* [After she told her therapist about someone who questioned her memories, her therapist] *became furious and told me he had no right to deny my pain. She said he should stick to his own profession and leave the therapy to her. . . . I had even been warned in healing books to avoid at all cost any psychiatrist or the like who expressed any doubt about the validity of my repressed memories of sexual abuse. It was dangerous to my emotional health to allow anyone to "deny my pain."*[43]

This woman was writing about a clergyman who questioned her R-memories after extended contact with her and her family. The principle applies to siblings, other family members, and spouses who do not believe. It is not enough to accept an R-memory with reservations about its truth; zealous therapists insist it must be believed in toto, on faith.

Divorced from family and friends, the client with R-memories is encouraged to develop a "family of choice" to replace their "unhealthy" family of origin. This usually means the group of peers that surround the therapy, i.e. other patients. Support groups of different kinds abound in the incest treatment movement, providing a feeling of belonging, connection and mutual support to its members. Unfortunately the acceptance of the group is typically contingent upon perceiving and describing oneself as having been abused! With family contact gone and few or no friends outside the movement, this becomes a powerful motive for staying in therapy, continuing to dredge for memories, holding on to the recovered memory ideology.

> [T]he flashbacks were not reality. And there is a definite payoff. At no other time in your life do you get the kind of attention, love, support, nurturing from group members, cards, letters, financial assistance, people feeling sorry for you, people calling to check on you, and much much more. We, the group members, clung to each other for our absolute existence. We sustained each other, many times keeping each other from harming ourselves or, in some cases, committing suicide. We became each other's family, just as we had been told we would.[44]

Retractors are disparaged in the movement:

> I also felt guilty in group when there was talk of a woman outside the group who had recanted her repressed memories of sexual abuse and had reunited with her family. She was spoken about as being weak and uncourageous.[45]

R-MEMORIES AND PSYCHOTHERAPY

Part of the allure and the damage done by deep involvement in memory recovery therapy is the support it so often gives to abdicating normal life responsibilities. A retractor became addicted to prescription drugs in the course of her therapy, and wrote about the difference there had been between her R-memory therapy and a treatment program for drug addiction:

> *They didn't want to hear much about the abuse. . . . Instead, they stressed, "What are you going to do about now? You can't drink today, you can't take pills. You have to do the normal things you used to do. So what, you're depressed today. . . . You still must go to work, you must eat, you still must take a bath. . . ."*
>
> *I'd never had therapy like that before. In my incest victimization therapy. . . . If I felt bad, I'd stay home. I'd stay in bed all day. I'd read a book. I'd bawl, I'd take an extra Xanax. I didn't have to be responsible. If I'd had kids I wouldn't have to take care of them because I'm an incest victim. Because all of these awful things happened to me I didn't have to live by the same rules as everyone else does.*[46]

Perhaps the most important piece of the puzzle of R-memory therapy is the money made through long-term therapy, whether involving genuine or confabulated memories. Thousands, even hundreds of thousands, of dollars have been spent by single individuals on their therapy. This is the main reason for the lawsuits some retractors file when they decide their memories are false. This is from the story of a retractor who was hospitalized, along with her two daughters:

> *We were fortunate to have excellent insurance with unlimited benefits. But that changed too. I received notification from the insurance company that effective January 1, 1993 there would be a limit of $150,000 lifetime maximum. That is when the doctors and therapists began to talk about discharge.*[47]

Much of the money involved comes from health insurance or government medical programs, a deep pocket of funds to support R-memory therapy. Therapists diagnose clients with various mental disorders that are accepted as requiring long-term therapy and can be paid for by insurance programs. "Insurance companies report an astonishing rise in claims for Post-Traumatic Stress Disorder or Multiple Personality Disorder," wrote *Newsday*, "almost all of which cite childhood sexual abuse as the cause."[48] The senior vice-president of the mental health arm of Aetna states, "claims for Post-Traumatic Stress Disorder have risen fivefold in the past five years, and ten times as many Multiple Personality Disorder claims are received than ten years ago." In one managed health care group, "thirty percent of the mental health costs were used by less than one percent of the participants. Two group-practitioners racked up nearly $2 million in costs in just a year. Most of this was for repressed memories and multiple personality."[49]

Making money may not be a conscious motive for therapists who foster pseudomemory development, but it does make the profession profitable and keep therapists in practice.

To quote Paul McHugh of Johns Hopkins again, from his article in the *American Scholar*:[50]

> During the last seven or eight years, another example of misidentified hysterical behavior has surfaced and again has been bolstered by an invented view of its cause that fits a cultural fashion. This condition is "Multiple Personality Disorder".... (p. 505)

> Sexual politics in the 1980s and 1990s, particularly those connected with sexual oppression and victimization, galvanizes these inventions. Forgotten sexual mistreatment in childhood is the most frequently proffered explanation of MPD. Just as an epidemic of bewitchment served to prove

> the arrival of Satan in Salem, so in our day an epidemic of MPD is used to confirm that a vast number of adults were sexually abused by guardians during their childhood. (p. 506)
>
> Just as the divines of Massachusetts were convinced that they were fighting Satan by recognizing bewitchment, so the contemporary divines—these are therapists—are confident that they are fighting perpetrators of a common expression of sexual oppression, child abuse, by recognizing MPD.
>
> The incidence of MPD has of late indeed taken on epidemic proportions, particularly in certain treatment centers. Whereas its diagnosis was reported less than two hundred times from a variety of supposed causes in the last century, it has been applied to more than 20,000 people in the last decade and largely attributed to sexual abuse. (p. 507)

Professor McHugh's article deserves reading in its entirety by those wishing to understand the larger issues surrounding R-memories and their therapy.

Therapists creating pseudomemories of sex abuse have a wide range of backgrounds and credentials. Some are M.D.'s or Ph.D.'s; some have very little formal training. They may work under the banner of feminist consciousness raising or therapy for Post-Traumatic Stress Disorder or for Multiple Personality Disorder, or hypnotherapy. They may be psychiatrists, psychologists, family or pastoral counselors, or even Radix teachers.[51] The application of Freud's discovery of pseudomemory development has provided a shot in the arm for certain professionals, who no longer have to find patients who actually remember being abused sexually. If they find patients who are suggestible, the technology is well developed to turn them into sex abuse victims who develop pseudo-memories of their abuse, recovered after ten, twenty, or thirty years of alleged amnesia.

Reflections on the Recovered Memory Therapy Movement

In retrospect, the extreme elements of the recovered memory therapy movement bear all the hallmarks of a cult. Retractors have found that seeing their experience of therapy as cult involvement explains well what they went through. A cult's belief system pervades every aspect of a follower's life, and can become quite irrational. Followers are systematically isolated from those who do not share the cult's belief systems. Any who leave the cult are disparaged. The cult-prescribed activities become more and more total, using more personal time and money as time goes by. Followers form close relationships only with other cult members. There is no clear path out of the cult situation. Parents are manipulated into giving money to the cult by paying for their children's therapy.

Surely there are many therapists working with victims of abuse who are careful and responsible, and do not involve themselves in the excesses found in the movement. To paint all psychotherapists, hypnotherapists, or other helping professionals working with victims of sex abuse as fostering pseudomemory would be as serious a mistake as claiming that all recovered memories are false or that all are true. But many qualified therapists use regressive and suggestive techniques that encourage pseudomemory. It is part of the search after trauma to "explain" a client's difficulties.

Psychotherapists greatly overemphasize traumas as causes of people's difficulties in life, mostly because they give something definite to hang a client's problems onto. R-memories of abuse provide a ready explanation for emotional difficulties and blocks. But blocked emotions are rarely caused by traumatic events. Instead, they develop in the day-after-day relationships of infant and child to significant others in life, the repeated occurrences of painful, frightening, or frustrating—and pleasurable, sometimes sexually tinged experiences—that make up most of one's emotional history. It is not the memory of such experiences, but the habitual muscular patterns, the armor, developed to block and control feelings evoked by these emotional events that is the dynamic element in work with the feelings. If the muscular armor is freed, blocked feelings will be released. The release may or may not be accompanied by a memory of a particular time when strong feelings were blocked, e.g., memory of a trauma. Reich found and we have confirmed that it doesn't matter to the course of freeing the blocked feelings if such memories are recovered or not. The freeing of the armor follows its own course in either event. The case history of Martha in Chapter Five illustrates the point, a case where there was a real, brutal, and remembered rape in childhood, a trauma that could have been wrongly blamed for that client's emotional problems.

Perhaps the most devastating effect of the excesses of R-memory psychotherapy is the suspicion it casts on those who report genuine memories of abuse. Knowing about the existence of pseudomemory, responsible professionals must meet R-memories of abuse with reserve and skepticism, yet with an open mind. As the truth about the excesses of irresponsible and naive therapists working with R-memories becomes better known, the same open-minded attitude becomes harder to maintain. Skepticism about abuse stories based on dubious R-memories may well extend to authentic cases of abuse—another swing of the pendulum back to disbelief. We must acknowledge that R-memories may be true, false, or garbled, and dismiss no one's experiences—including experiences of memories—lightly.

There is a growing backlash against therapists in general, and against R-memory work with sexual abuse in particular. Already popular press articles focussed on cases of false memory cast general aspersions on therapy as a whole.[52] Psychotherapy and the R-memory therapy movement have some lumps to take, but to dismiss therapy entirely is to throw a beautiful baby out with the bathwater. Responsible, careful, dedicated professionals, devoted to helping people with personal problems, deserve better than that. But it is time for them to speak up on this problem in their profession.

4

R-Memories of Ritual Abuse and Alien Abduction

The same techniques used in developing R-memories of sex abuse in therapy can lead to "memories" of other kinds of events, some of them quite fantastic. I have had Radix students who as a consequence of therapy of some kind "remembered" their own birth, others who "recalled" conversations between their parents before birth (i.e., heard in utero), others still who recovered "memories" of one or more past lives. There is a substantial literature on recovered memories of abductions onto UFOs and sex abuse at the hands of alien beings. "Satanic ritual abuse" involving R-memories of murder, cannibalism, and devil worship as well as sexual abuse, is a well-defined area already mentioned. Many of these memories were obtained by hypnotic or highly suggestive regressive techniques. The various "recovered memories" are often detailed, vivid, and experienced with the profound conviction of their authenticity.

The clarity, vividness, or strength of the conviction that an R-memory is authentic is not good evidence that the remembered event really happened. This is as true of recovered memories of childhood sexual abuse, physical abuse, and satanic horrors as it is of recovered memories of birth, prebirth, past life, and UFO abduction experiences. The process of memory recovery in each type of case is often quite similar. Skilled suggestive probing for repressed memories by therapists in search of memories of sex abuse or of past lives or of abductions by extraterrestrials is all too apt to "succeed." The R-memories produced in these "far out" areas show how R-memories can be produced by suggestion in the presence of a well-developed belief system. We who do not believe in large-scale abductions by extraterrestrials or in past lives can only conclude that these R-memories are objectively false, a consequence of the techniques giving rise to them and the belief system supporting them.

Satanic Ritual Abuse (SRA)

Michelle Remembers, by M. Smith and L. Pazder,[53] a tale of satanic ritual abuse, is to my mind the model description of the growth of pseudomemories in regressive therapy. As is usually the case, Michelle's R-memories of abuse in her therapy are progressive, becoming more and more strange. Eventually she is remembering being forced to participate in evil satanic rites, including sexual rites, animal and infant sacrifice, and other horrors. She feels evil inside herself, and eventually goes to the Roman Catholic Church to have the evil exorcised. I would have titled the book *Michelle Confabulates*.

The Fall 1992 *Journal of Psychology and Theology*, an evangelical Christian publication,[54] is devoted entirely to the current state of knowledge of satanic ritual abuse. Martha Rogers is the guest editor for this issue. It includes some thirty-plus articles and rejoinders, including, to the editor's credit, a good representation of articles from outside the evangelical community. The editor's introductory article and selected annotated bibliography are even-handed and thoughtful. I can't say as much for many of the contributions. Some are quite crazy, in my estimation.

Satanic abuse gets lots of media attention. How extensive is it really? How often do SRA clients appear in psychotherapy offices? Bottoms et al., in a paper to the 1991 American Psychological Association (APA), which was reviewed in some detail by the guest editor in the journal described above, gives some answers.[55] The authors mailed a survey on the subject to clinical psychologists who were members of the APA. Their survey questionnaire asked about clients coming into therapy with satanic ritual abuse or other religion-related abuse issues since the year 1980. Seventy percent of the respondents had seen no such cases at all. The majority of the remaining thirty percent had seen one case. Most of these were not satanic, but abuse by an official with a public religious affiliation, e.g., a priest or minister. However, sixteen psychologists, comprising six-tenths of one percent of the 2,709 respondents, each reported having seen from one hundred to two thousand religious abuse cases, most of them involving satanism. In other words, satanic ritual abuse cases are seen very rarely in psychotherapy, mostly by a handful of therapists specializing in the area. In our opinion, the vast majority of satanic abuse cases are created by regressive techniques of memory recovery employed by therapists within an extreme fundamentalist Christian belief system. Pseudomemories develop that incorporate religious fantasies about the devil as the active agent producing many of the problems for which people seek psychotherapy. Others surface in clients with dissociative tendencies who slip into regressive states spontaneously. It may happen alone or with a therapist who is not intentionally employing regressive techniques but is not effective at preventing it.

Psychologists Ruth E. Shaffer, of the Psychiatry Department of the Harbor-UCLA Medical Center, and Louis J. Cozolino, of Pepperdine University, report interviews of twenty subjects who in their therapy recovered "memories" of satanic ritual abuse.[56] The subjects' ages ranged from twenty to fifty-three. Nineteen of the twenty were women. They entered therapy with similar complaints: emotional problems, dissociation, body complaints, eating disorders. One had reported a vague intimation of satanic abuse. The other nineteen had no intimation of such things when they entered therapy.

With the primary focus of therapy being the uncovering of memories, these were the developments:

> All subjects reported witnessing the sacrificial murder of animals, infants, children, and/or adults. Corpses were often subjected to sexual violations and cannibalistic feasting. The vast majority of subjects in this study reported severe and sadistic forms of sexual abuse by multiple perpetrators. . . .
>
> . . . Unwillingness to partake in the torture and murder of others resulted in severe reprisals for non-compliance that included being suspended on hooks from walls and ceilings; having arms and legs twisted; being given electric shocks; having hair and body parts burned; and confinement to coffins that often contained insects, spiders, and snakes. . . .
>
> . . . All reported suicidal ideation; half reported repeated suicide attempts. Of all the subjects, 55 percent reported repeated psychiatric hospitalizations during the initial and middle stages of psychotherapy.
>
> Participation in twelve-step programs as well as support groups such as Incest Survivors Anonymous, Victims Anonymous, and Adults Molested as Children was reported by the majority as necessary adjuncts to psychotherapy. This served to provide virtual substitute families for many victims who had cut ties with their biological families as a result of either their disclosures of earlier abuse being met with denial and/or discovering that the families were cult involved. (pp. 189-190)

The following is from a clinical vignette said to characterize the average range of experiences of the subjects:

> Jan sought therapy at the age of 27.... Over a span of six years and nine months, she consulted with five psychotherapists and was variously diagnosed with Major Depression, Adjustment Disorder, Bipolar Disorder with Psychotic Features, Schizophrenia, and Multiple Personality Disorder....
>
> ... [W]ith the help of her fifth therapist [the fourth, fifth, and sixth year of treatment], Jan uncovered memories of ritualistic abuse by her father, her maternal grandparents, maternal uncles and aunts, and family acquaintances, abuse that she believed began in infancy and had continued to the age of 16. She had been amnesic for these events for over 20 years....
>
> During Jan's fifth and sixth year of therapy, she surfaced memories of sexual abuse with foreign objects, forced sex with animals, and ritualistic abuse during adolescence. More recently, she has surfaced extremely painful memories of being impregnated and giving birth at the age of 14 to an infant who was sacrificed, dismembered, and consumed....
>
> ... The primary focus of the therapy continues to be on the uncovering of memories.... Although the uncovering of memories, at times, continues to elicit some deterioration that manifests itself in suicidal ideation and self-mutilation, for Jan, these now occur less frequently and are of shorter duration. Literature on sexual abuse, participation in victim's groups, writing, and artwork have been helpful resources outside of therapy. (pp. 190-192)

This article represents the viewpoint and work of "true believers" in satanic ritual abuse, and their way of working with it. We didn't go on to include the reports of emergence of Multiple Personality Disorder in their case history. We consider this case to be an example of the horrors of pseudomemory generation using regressive techniques of "memory" recovery. The client is the victim, not of a satanic cult of abusers but of the therapist. It is the "reductio ad absurdum" of Freud's discovery of the pseudomemories that are produced by the regression of hysteric clients. It shows the effects when therapists work with these memories as if they are real, in the context of a supporting belief system.

If the monstrous crimes reported by clients "remembering" satanic abuse really happened, there would be hard evidence. Ceremonies involving murder leave bones. Torture, including electric shocks, or being hung on hooks or burned or whipped, leaves marks. Most of all, conspiracies involving numbers of people engaged in felonious activities have defectors. They are infiltrated by the FBI and other law enforcement groups. Even the most powerful crime organizations slip up. The FBI and other agencies have investigated satanic ritual abuse allegations. Except for the occasional demented individual and a few who are their hangers-on for a time, they have nothing to support the charges.

Believers tell a different story. They write of superpowerful criminals engaged in SRA who commit perfect crime after perfect crime—murder, torture, rape—year after year. They recognize that this could only happen with the help of a superbeing with extra-human powers, i.e., Satan, who, they claim, has powerful accomplices in law enforcement and other government agencies helping his followers cover up these nefarious crimes.

Those who believe these fantastic tales are the true cultists. There is no hard evidence that there is any multi-generational satanic conspiracy engaged in ritual murder, cannibalism, rape, child sacrifices, etc. SRA is the creation of those who have been persuaded to believe in such things. In particular, it is the creation of psychotherapists encouraging pseudomemory through intense regressive fantasies, abetted by sects of religious zealots believing in Satan and his power.

Alien Abductions

Those who follow such things say there are more people who report being abducted by aliens from outer space than who report satanic ritual abuse experiences. The victims are spirited through walls, ceilings, and closed windows to alien space ships and back. The aliens can paralyze people and turn off machinery with a thought. They are not one intelligent race of beings contacting another, but superbeings using a lower order of being (us) as they wish to advance purposes they do not make clear, but presumably having to do with breeding and cross-breeding with humans. That is the story.

SRA and alien abduction stories show great similarities. Both experiences bring amnesia, it is claimed, gaps in memory, to be filled in by regressive and often hypnotic techniques of memory recovery. Both involve superpowerful beings who exercise mind control. Satanists derive their superhuman powers through alliance with an evil religious superbeing or beings; space aliens are said to derive their superhuman powers from an alien super-science far in advance of our own. Satanists perform their rituals in service to the powers of evil. Aliens perform medical and scientific experiments on their hapless victims, operating on them, taking eggs and sperm from their bodies, forcing them to surrender the contents of their minds telepathically and to have sex with other abductees through their mind control, and to endure other violations. The space aliens visit and abduct the same people again and again—their experimental subjects.

There is only the slightest hard evidence of their existence. No abductee has brought back any convincing artifacts or photographs of their captors and their civilization. They are said, like the satanists, to have powerful allies in military, space, and law enforcement agencies. They conspire to hide government knowledge of the space aliens and their craft from us.

How do we know about the space aliens and their experiments? The amnesias that their mind control produces are imperfect, we are told. Abductees have gaps of time in their lives, and intimations that something is going on that they don't understand. They find their way to therapists who deal in such things. These therapists, with the help of hypnotic regression, help them discover their R-memories of alien abduction, and therapists and clients write books. I have read these books since the 1950s, and was for years a member of NICAP, the National Committee for the Investigation of Aerial Phenomena, then the major UFO sightings organization. The details of abduction stories differ a good deal, but have gradually converged toward the story we have described here.[57]

Belief Systems and Pseudomemories of Sexual Abuse

Pseudomemories of abuse have been with us for centuries. At the time of the witchcraft trials of the sixteenth and seventeenth centuries, they were interpreted under the more general category of religious abuse and abominations, where some religious believers in satanism try to keep them today. At the time of the witchcraft trials, children and other highly suggestible people lived with the belief that there were witches, direct agents of Satan, among them. Inquisitors elicited pseudomemories from children and others, often young girls, of accused witches flying, turning into animals, and performing horrible abusive devilish acts. The witches were convicted on the basis of such evidence and many were burned alive or drowned. At that time, the active evil agents of witchcraft were said to be mostly women. The active evil agents of incestuous abuse and satanic ritual abuse today are said to be mostly men.

Pseudomemories of alien abduction and abuse take place within a different belief system, one of a "superscience," the product of beings coming from planetary systems unknown to us. The world of science fiction has evolved this new mythology that is acceptable to many to whom a belief in Satan and his superpowers would seem naive and silly.

The belief system of the intermediaries of R-memories of sex abuse today has two main roots. The feminist root lies in the struggle of women for a more equitable role in society, a struggle which most men support. However, the zealots of feminism have articulated a far more extreme belief system under the banner of feminism in which women are held to be an oppressed victim class, badly misused by men, deliberately kept in a powerless child-like role in society, and subjected to widespread criminal sexual abuse. Such abuse is said to be much more widespread than official statistics show, particularly when women are young and powerless to prevent it. Pseudomemories of sex abuse by powerful male perpetrators fit perfectly into the feminist zealot's belief system.

The second belief system supporting the production of pseudomemories of childhood sexual abuse is that which legitimizes and supports the overextension of therapy in dealing with the problems and distresses of living. Some therapists create ever new and expanding categories of mental illnesses people can be diagnosed to be suffering from, treatment of which can be paid for through health insurance or government medical programs. Post-Traumatic Stress Disorder (PTSD) and Multiple Personality Disorder (MPD) are current favorites of the therapy industry. These frequently involve R-memories of incestuous abuse.

With their pseudomemories certified as genuine by their therapists, pseudomemory victims are encouraged to act on them, accusing parents and other family members of the horrible crimes their therapy "revealed." It is a modern form of prosecution for witchcraft that villainizes the accused, often without a shred of hard evidence. It even shares the spotlight with the old form of belief in witchcraft, now operating under the label of satanic ritual abuse. These travesties of psychotherapy are made possible by the belief systems that form their context, and by R-memory therapists who accept the belief system and carry out the intermediating that produces the pseudomemories. Subjects have the willing assistance of lawyers who have everything to gain from a successful suit against the alleged perpetrator. The existence of as much true childhood sex abuse as there is masks the many cases based on pseudomemories that are now lumped with them. Legitimate psychotherapists who do not speak out bear a responsibility for the growth of these practices.

Pseudomemories become a widespread group phenomenon when they are seized on by the supporters of a belief system as evidence of the validity of that system. In themselves, pseudomemories are nothing more and nothing less than vivid R-memories of deep, usually sexual and sex-related fantasies, myths, artifacts of therapists' agendas, distorted fragments of true memories, and dreams of highly suggestible individuals. Zealots supporting the system may then bring together the belief system and the suggestible individuals in a way that promotes the pseudomemories as evidence for that system's beliefs. Their skill lies in inducing and molding their subjects' pseudomemories into a form that supports their beliefs, and in creating a way of getting paid for their efforts. They were once the inquisitors of witnesses to witchcraft. These evolved into fundamentalist psychotherapists treating satanic ritual abuse. Today they are Post-Traumatic Stress Disorder and Multiple Personality Disorder therapists, hypnotherapists, and other therapists employing hypnotic and other suggestive techniques for producing R-memories of incest. Many are paid for through health insurance systems.

Under the skilled and purposive guidance of the zealot intermediaries and their cohorts supporting their system of belief, then, vivid fantasies that become the basis of pseudomemories are born.

Intermediaries would like the world to believe that the often similar stories of R-memories, be they of UFO abductions, satanism, sex abuse by evil family members, or past lives, are true accounts of what subjects remember, facilitated by the intermediaries but not influenced in their content. The role of the intermediaries, however, and the belief system they bring to their work, is absolutely central to the content subjects produce in all these areas. This role was demonstrated dramatically in a different context by the following experiment bearing on the suspected childhood sex abuse of autistic children.

Autism and Intermediaries

Some scholars have held that autism is psychogenic, caused by trauma, perhaps reflecting a history of abuse. Most experts believe it to be a congenital neuromuscular disorder that causes a severe impairment of intellectual function. Some autistic subjects show exceptional ability in narrow areas, as in drawing from memory, or in making mental calculations as portrayed by Dustin Hoffman in *Rain Man*. An apparent breakthrough in communication with autistic people has created a great deal of discussion among interested professionals in recent years. It appeared that the autistic child could learn to communicate more normally with the help of "facilitators"—trained intermediaries—and a computer. In this "facilitated communication," autistic subjects learned to communicate through a keyboard much more clearly and at a higher level of intellectual ability than ever possible before. The system employs individual facilitators who are in physical contact with the autistic subjects so that they can help subjects overcome patterns of neuromuscular tension that arise to block the keyboard responses their autistic subjects are trying to make. By freeing these tensions, facilitated keyboard communication seems to bring greatly improved communication with the autistic.

Retarded children and adults are known sometimes to be the victims of sex abuse by family and other caretakers. The facilitated communication system provided a tool for investigating sex abuse histories of the autistic. It resulted in evidence of widespread and frequent abuse of these unfortunate handicapped victims, abuse denied by families involved. A carefully controlled experiment was then done to test the facilitators' role in the communication process. The experiment showed that the responses of the autistic subjects were unconsciously cued by the facilitators.[58] The evidence of abuse was entirely the product of the facilitators, who were not previously known to influence the content of the facilitated communication. All of the children's facilitated responses through their computer keyboards proved to be signaled unconsciously by their facilitators, who were the intermediaries through which evidence of abuse had come. There was no genuine evidence from the children of sex abuse in the computer-assisted communications they made, and no real evidence of improved communication by autistic subjects. The study was featured in the PBS television program *Frontline*.

The facts are clear. Some autistic and other mentally handicapped individuals are sexually abused; this we know in advance. What was learned was that intermediaries, in this case trained facilitators who believe there is sex abuse in a given case, unconsciously produce false evidence of such abuse and attribute it entirely to their subjects. And this is precisely what happens with the therapists who are the intermediaries in cases of alien abductions, satanic ritual abuse, and pseudomemories of sex abuse recovered as a consequence of therapy.

However, it must always be remembered that while space aliens and tales of Satan are fantasies, sex abuse of children (and the handicapped) is real and widespread, and *some* recovered memories of abuse are true in whole or in part. Nonetheless, therapists are producing false evidence of childhood sex abuse on a widespread basis through techniques of memory "recovery."

There is another related phenomenon. A number of day-care operators and teachers have been accused and some convicted of sexually abusing the children under their care. In California the staff of the McMartin day school were legally charged with sexually molesting children in their care, and with performing satanic rituals. After months and months of testimony from teachers, therapists, and every kind of expert in what was said to be the longest and most expensive trial in California history, the jury did not convict anyone on any of the many charges made. It appears that the McMartin stories of sex abuse and satanism came mainly from the leading questions of social workers who conducted the questioning after a parent's complaint. In our opinion social workers served as intermediaries unconsciously creating pseudomemories of abuse. Children, autistic or not, are very responsive to suggestion. Perhaps some children were mistreated at the McMartin school, perhaps not. In the mass of confusion spread by suggestive questioning, the accused could not be convicted in good conscience. The school was of course destroyed, the reputation of the family that ran it ruined.

Other day school cases worked out still less fortunately. Operators of the Little Rascals day school in North Carolina were convicted of abuse on the basis of the opinions of therapists who saw the children after certain parents suspected abuse. The individual therapy sessions which led to the court action were not videotaped, so it was not recorded what was asked of the children or how. However, the therapists' notes, documenting the opinions formed that the children were abused, were supplied to the jury, and leading questions of the children were permitted by the court, allowing the prosecutors to all but put words in the children's mouths, convicting the accused. The proprietor of the school and one of his teachers are in prison as a result. It is at least possible that those convicted were entirely innocent of the abuse of which they were accused, and are the victims of today's form of witchcraft persecution just as the witches were, out of the mouths of children. There are other day-care cases.

To summarize, only a few centuries ago, intermediaries helped children remember accused witches, sometimes members of the child's own family, turn into animals, fly, and commit heinous sins against God. Today, therapist intermediaries help subjects "discover" that they have been abducted by aliens for sex experiments, participated in satanic rites involving forced sex, murder, and cannibalism, that autistic children have been sexually abused, that day school teachers have used their charges in satanic ritual acts and abused them in other ways, and that many parents have sexually abused their children who, it is claimed, developed complete or partial amnesia for the happening until adulthood, when the intermediaries' help was obtained.

It would seem that some measure of skepticism is in order in dealing with such stories.

5

Dealing with Memories of Incestuous Abuse

Sexual abuse by an older family member is one of the most difficult things for a child to handle. Children subject to such abuse have to deal with it the best they can. Who they tell (if anyone) and the response they receive may help them or add further to the problem. The child's knowledge is limited, and options are few. The fortunate ones receive appropriate help when they need it, and are able to integrate their negative experiences into their growth and development. But for many, the memory and aftereffects remain as unfinished business. At some point in adulthood, they may interfere with the victim's life enough that they need to be dealt with.

Having been incestuously abused in childhood does not comprise a form of mental illness or neurosis. Even though it can be a shocking or painful experience, it is not in and of itself a determinant of the character of the adult. Some people of all character types are subject to incestuous abuse. They do not form a diagnostic category. If a victim of incestuous abuse should elect to go to a psychotherapist, there is no branch or specialty in psychotherapy that exists especially to deal with them. Those claiming to specialize in "incest recovery" require careful screening.

They may be specialists in producing R-memories.

There are cases of childhood incestuous abuse among the clients of virtually any established psychotherapy practice because such abuse is common. It is not usually why people come to psychotherapy, though it is often one contributing factor. Ideally, a prospective client with an incest history will find a broadly-based, reality-oriented, group psychotherapy practice which has a balance of men and women clients and which includes effective body work. There are other forms of useful therapy, of course. Group work and good body work are mentioned because they may be especially useful to clients who have a history of abuse. For those wishing to talk about their abuse experience but not seeking psychotherapy, leaderless both-sex groups, twelve-step programs, or other member-run programs can be good when there is no axe to grind or ideology pushing the group, and when a firm commitment is a condition of participation. All groups need that condition to be effective. Our advice to childhood incest victims is that they find a way to deal with it if they haven't, without making either more nor less of it than it is. Those needing professional help should investigate possible therapists, and find out how they actually work. It takes time and care to find a good one. There are further suggestions later in this chapter.

Continuous (Normal) Memories of Incestuous Abuse

In the great majority of cases, childhood incest is clearly and vividly remembered in adulthood, though events surrounding the experience may be murky or lost to memory. And whereas the child had few options, the adult has several. As a minimum, sober adult consideration of what happened back then, and measures to help the processing may be called for, e.g., discussing what happened with the abuser in certain cases, or with other family members, a friend, or a professional counselor. Sometimes action may

DEALING WITH MEMORIES OF INCESTUOUS ABUSE

be called for to prevent abuse of others, even though the original abuse occurred long ago.

> *A woman had undergone intense explicitly sexual fondling from her father from the age of five to seven. Nothing had been said about it to anyone at the time it happened or in the intervening years, but her memory of the abuse and the upset and problems it caused her was clear, vivid, and uninterrupted. When she was twenty-six she learned that her older brother and his wife were planning to go to Europe for five weeks, leaving their little girl of five with the grandparents, her and her brother's parents. The woman was afraid that the child would suffer the same kind of abuse from her father that she had been exposed to at his hands when she was the same age.*

It's easy for us as outsiders to offer advice. The young woman should tell her brother and sister-in-law exactly what happened twenty years before, and recommend strongly that their daughter not be left alone with the abusing grandparent. It is never that simple, however. She did tell, and—

> *The brother didn't believe his younger sister and her twenty-years-after-the-fact memories. He had for some years considered her to be something of a "flake." The sister-in-law did believe her, at least to the extent that she wouldn't leave the child as planned. Word as to why got back to the mother, who had looked forward to taking care of the grandchild, had had a little playground set up in her backyard, etc. A family crisis ensued, involving grandparents, their son, daughter and daughter-in-law. The daughter-in-law set up a meeting of them all with a family systems therapist, which they all agreed to attend. When the time for the meeting arrived, the grandfather would not go, in a way that convinced his wife of his guilt. The meeting helped the others clear their feelings and reaffirm their mutual bonds. But the family was not, and will probably never*

again, be the same.

A few weeks after the meeting the young woman took a courageous step. She went to see her father alone. She told him that she loved him, and how important he always was in her life. Then she told him about how it affected her when he came in and fondled her sexually when she was a little girl, how deeply it upset and frightened her, how it confused her sexually and took her years to come to terms with. She told him that she did want to keep him in her life, but that if she ever had children, she would never leave them alone with him—that was a condition of their relationship. He apologized, acknowledged that the blame was entirely his, and she left him crying.

That young woman did the difficult things her situation called for and, in so doing, dealt with her memory of incestuous sexual abuse.

Incestuous abuse of a child leaves not only memories and loss of trust, it also leaves effects on the body. Like other emotional experiences, it helps produce or intensify chronic patterns of muscular tension blocking emotions and sexual feelings. These are the character defenses embedded in the body. Wilhelm Reich discovered these patterns of tension and called them the "muscular armor."[59] Patterns of muscular armor tied to early sexual experience may affect the child into adult life. If fortunate, as an adolescent or young adult the abused child will become able to love, to trust, and to surrender sexually, and this muscular armor will soften away. Often, however, abuse intensifies the pre-existing muscular armor. The fear or pain or anger held back from expression by the armor becomes less available and harder to reach. It is a mistake for the professional working with such cases to overfocus on the memory of abuse. It is the blocks in the body, the whole pattern of muscular and character armor, that is the problem, not the memories. Here is an example from my Radix neo-Reichian practice:

Martha was a thirty-two-year old, rather thin social worker, with reddish hair and freckled skin. Bright and "heady," she had done some fifty sessions with me over a year-and-a-half period. Sex abuse was one of her issues. She had been raped by her stepfather when she was twelve, while her mother was sleeping heavily from drink and drugs, as she thought he had planned. She had talked about it with me frankly, but still had too many upper body tensions—muscular armorings—to deal with her deep pelvic feelings. (Upper-body tensions are dealt with first in Radix body work.) She was getting closer to the pelvic material. In her sessions with me, she had worked through eye and jaw and throat blocks, which would reassert when she was frightened, but she had become able to stay present better with her fear.

She lay on her back on the mat that I use in doing bodywork and I knelt beside her. I helped her keep in contact and open, breathing freely and connecting with me through her eyes. We were doing some work to free her chest and diaphragm, which had released further than usual. Suddenly she tightened and fear came into her eyes. I moved my hands instinctively to her jaw and the back of her neck.

"What's the thought?" I asked.

"It's when he raped me," she said. Her neck was tightening, her jaw pulling back.

"Stay with the feelings that are there right now. Don't push back into the memory, but stay with what you feel, and keep aware of where we are, in this room."

I worked to keep her present with me yet surrendering to the rising fear, which increased as I helped her to release muscles that blocked it. I put pressure on the tense muscles of her neck and jaw. "Breathe," I said and, with the pressure from my forearm on her chest, encouraged her to exhale. As I worked the back of her neck and her jaw with fingers and thumb, I had her *make loud sounds into my eyes. Suddenly there was a release. The fear escalated. The pupils of her eyes dilated, the sounds rose toward a scream, the back of the neck went into hard recontraction, the eyes froze open wide in terror. I struggled to free the neck.*

"Stay with me," I ordered, "Kick, and let the scream reach higher." (The kicking might loosen some of the pelvic tension.) I gripped the hair on the top of her head and shook it to loosen the scalp, tight with fear, while she kicked. The screams then seemed to go to the very top of her skull. Piercing, hair-raising, they made my ears ring. I wrestled against the neck contracting, struggled to keep her in her eyes. It seemed a long time, but I know the discharge was no more than twenty seconds. Then the sounds subsided, and her body shook as it began to relax.

"Stay in the room, Martha," I said. "Keep seeing me, and the room we're in."

But she was seeing me. The pupils of her eyes had come back to normal size, her face was relaxing, her shoulders let down, and her breathing became easy. There was a most striking change in expression taking place in her eyes and mouth. She was present in a way she had never been before.—She was with herself, in her body and with me. She looked at me directly, with a kind of curiosity. "You're not so scary," she said, and she smiled an unforced and different smile, more self-possessed than I'd ever seen her. She had gotten through a piece of her blocked fear, a significant piece. Later I would bring up her rape. It was less important. Letting go of some of her fear armor—that was important. She told me she did not relive the rape during the fear discharge, though its memory triggered the fear process.

The secret of effective work with the armor blocking the feelings is to keep the client present while surrendering to the feelings. It is much easier for clients to close their eyes (or shut down visual awareness with the eyes open), and sink into memory or fantasy images that produce fear and support their fear armor than to stay present as they release the armor and let the fear develop spontaneously. Feelings produced by fantasy or old memories may be expressed actively and loudly. They look impressive to those who don't know any better, but they do no long-term good. The feelings are being cranked up by the memory or fantasy, but the armor is not released, it is tightening. The memories are not being integrated into present experience as they occur. Clients must be aware of who they are and where they are as the armor releases and the feelings happen for the emotional discharge to mean anything. It is the awareness of present time, place and situation that forms the bridge to reality for the feelings released by the armor. People can regress into a childhood memory of terror, rage or pain (sex abuse experiences are usually all three) again and again and again. Nothing changes. It's like playing to oneself repeated scary or enraging or painful movies of one's past life. The armor is not released by such exercises. But once the armor is released they experience the feelings in relation to present-time reality, as Martha did. Then they change. The release may or may not trigger old memories. It doesn't make any difference.

After her session with me, Martha was no longer afraid in the same way. Before it was as if she always carried the subterranean fear with her, a ghost from her past, which she connected to her rape. Now the ghost had been exorcised and she could, at last, take a deep breath and let herself be fully in the world. There was more work ahead, including work on her pelvic segment armor and related issues, but she'd taken a big step with this session.

Was Martha's fear really "caused" by the rape?—Only in part, although the rape became a focus of her fear process. Blocks to feelings are rarely created by single isolated traumas. Instead they build gradually in the day by day life of infant and child. The patterns of armor that play such a major part in character development are a product of the continuing interaction of child with family, and with significant others. Martha had a fear block, developed and exercised on hundreds of fear-laden occasions, long before the rape. The rape was especially terrifying, and came to represent her whole set of fears.

I worked, not with Martha's memory of rape per se, then, but with the fear block in her body which the memory of the rape represented. The significant change occurred because Martha became able in her session to release a pattern of muscular armor blocking her fear process. The release allowed Martha to experience the fear, which rose to the level of terror. *It was keeping open and present in her body as the fear came out* that was the significant part of the session. Whether or not the memory was present during discharge or after did not matter.

Suppose I had worked with Martha in a regressive way. When she mentioned the rape to me I could have had her close her eyes, let go of everything else on her mind and sink back into her memory of that night twenty years before. I could have helped her create the details of what happened and how she had felt moment by moment during the assault, the terror when he came in, sat on the bed where she had been sleeping, covered her mouth with his hand and warned her to make no sound; his alcoholic breath as he stripped the blanket from her bed, etc., helping her recreate the details of her ordeal moment by moment, one feeling response at a time. Such a regressive exercise would have intensified, not freed, the fear block in Martha's structure, especially that in her ocular segment. Even if I had encouraged her to scream during the regressive memory, and after the memory helped her into anger exercises to mobilize her petrified body and redirect her life force outward, the whole approach is of dubious value. She could do that kind of regressive exercise on her rape three times a week for many years, and not show a significant softening of the armor, the fear defenses. Cranking up the feelings via regressive exercises, aided by hypnosis or not, is not the same as releasing the armor process through body work such as Radix, properly applied. It is in an important respect an opposite way of working.

Twenty years ago the popular form of regressive feeling work was primal therapy. There were many ex-primal patients in my practice, and I compared primal regressive feeling work with Radix feeling work as follows:[60]

Radix Personal Growth Work	*Regressive Therapy*
Eyes open and seeing; outward and inward awareness present	Eyes closed or unseeing; outward awareness cut off
Feeling reactions arise as body armor is loosened	Feeling reactions arise from stimulation of emotional memories and fantasies
Contact with the here-and-now is sustained during emotional discharge	Contact with the here-and-now is cut off during emotional discharge
Frees the ocular armor segment	Intensifies armor in the ocular segment
Emotional reactions become more appropriate to real events	Emotional reactions become less appropriate to real events
Armor around the body core is decreased	Armor around the body core is increased
Interest in and frequency of sexual experience is increased.	Interest in and frequency of sexual experience is reduced.

The comparison remains valid today, even though the well-trained "incest recovery" therapist mixes regressive work with a variety of other techniques. The effect of therapy that relies on regressive techniques is the same now as then. Unfortunately, much of the work done today in the incest recovery field involving recovered memory of trauma, of sex abuse and satanic ritual abuse in particular, is regressive. In my opinion, most such work is profoundly anti-therapeutic. The feelings are excited without being freed, and true memories confounded and often lost in pseudomemory. The last four items on the right in the list above accurately describe the long term results of extensive regressive therapy.

Dealing with Recovered Memories

The examples and principles involved in dealing with the effects of continuously remembered abuse are simple and straightforward compared with cases involving recovered memories. Similar principles apply to working with R-memories as with continuous memories, but with complications. In the above two examples, the memories were normal and intact. The essential facts of the remembered abuse were never in question. They had their meaning in the reality of what happened, and dealing with them was dealing with the incest and its aftermath, its effect on victim, abuser, and family. This is the case with the overwhelming majority of abuse. The abuse takes place, makes an indelible impression, is remembered, and can be dealt with.

In R-memories of childhood abuse the situation is different. *The essential facts of abuse recalled in R-memories are always in question.* That is because R-memories are not part of the normal process of memory nor of normal repression (see Chapter Two). Those who have in adulthood recovered memories of childhood incestuous abuse must find for themselves how they will deal with them. Should they believe or doubt them? Professionals, no matter how skilled, are presumptuous to tell someone their memories are true or are false, though they are wise to urge caution. The professional is not omniscient. A person with R-memories of incestuous abuse should leave doors open in the mind. Once more we repeat, R-memories may be true as remembered; they may be garbled and incorrectly recalled, as when a person involved is mistakenly identified; and they may be false, the result of fantasies that were so convincing they became real in the mind. Facts about these matters are in this book. A person should not give away the power of decision as to whether one's R-memories are true or false to someone else. If the person knows that his or her own thought processes are impaired when the memories surface, judgment should be suspended until the head becomes clear. This can take years when dissociation is advanced. Clarity may be encouraged, however, by talking to friends or by seeing a professional with no axe to grind or position to defend, one who does not use hypnosis or regression to dredge for memories or otherwise contribute to a dissociative tendency. The objective is to clear one's own head. The need is to be free of pressure as to what to conclude. It is possible that one will never know for sure. Not knowing is better than "knowing" incorrectly.

How can one find the "right" professional help? People find the right mental health professional the same way they decide what college to go to or what lawyer to trust. They check around, use the Yellow Pages and the local mental health/bodywork resource guides, make inquiries, and use the knowledge they have. The searcher needs to take time, interview prospects, and read what they have written. Licenses and credentials mean very little in this area. Many "incest recovery" and "satanic ritual abuse" therapists that we could never recommend have impeccable credentials. Some unlicensed therapists, body workers and group leaders do good work. *It is essential to look into what they actually do.*

Those who understand the problems of recovered memories of abuse know that dealing with R-memories per se is a small part of what is needed. What is entailed is freeing the blocked feelings that the memories may have come to represent, and developing a reasonable balance between feeling and thinking, and between fantasy and reality, in daily life.

Even a false R-memory has a meaning of some kind. It is not created just because of extremist ideologies and incompetent or venal therapists. Consider those having pseudomemories or vivid fantasies of childhood incest (and the two shade into each other). When these are not the product of therapist suggestion, they are something to be dealt with by client and therapist. Why would an incest story surface spontaneously in someone's memory if it were not true? I have known of R-memories of incest and satanic abuse, memories that could not have been true, that appeared in the practice of professionals that did not encourage regression and did not suggest or welcome the horrors that poured out, but merely tried to work honestly with the material the client presented. How is one—client or therapist—to work with patently false memories that are important to the rememberer and carry a sense of significance with them?

Consider the simplest kind of case first. There is sometimes an unspoken and often unconscious undertone of sexuality in the relationship of father and daughter with no overt sex play or inappropriate touching. The child might be sensitive to her father's hidden thoughts and, as an adult exposed to "memory recovery" beliefs and techniques in therapy, produce an R-memory of incest. The memory itself is false, but accurately catches something in the feeling tone of father to daughter. Such feelings of father for daughter are very common and, if not acted on, innocent. The reverse, sexual feelings and fantasies of daughter to father (or son to mother) are virtually universal at one period in the normal development of the child's sexuality. Thus while the daughter's R-memory is false, it contains a significant element of truth. If the daughter has a wise therapist, the appearance of the R-memory or fantasy of incest can be an important step for the daughter toward understanding her relationship with her father. *Sometimes her fa-*

ther had sexual feelings toward her, and it affected their relationship. She was just a little girl and couldn't understand.

The wise therapist will help a client with R-memories work with the underlying feelings, without forcing the interpretation that R-memories are false *or* assuming they are true. It is best to share with the client that long forgotten memories of incest are common, and may or may not be literally true. The underlying feelings can nonetheless be processed without either besmirching innocent fathers and poisoning the client's family relationships or discounting what could turn out to be true R-memories of incest after all.

The mythical truths in R-memories and fantasies of incest are a rich field of work for professionals equipped to deal with them. It need not imply that a given R-memory is either false or true. Given that client and therapist recognize the difference between fantasy and reality, R-memories of incest can be analyzed and interpreted like a dream, using Freudian or Jungian techniques, or can be Gestalted, a la Fritz Perls,[61] to understand better their underlying feeling content. The work can also wander far from reality if R-memories become too large a part of the therapeutic process. But treating them as personal myth is a significant way of dealing with all kinds of R-memories. It is of particular value for strange and exotic memories of satanism, abduction by aliens, or scenes from "past lives."

The Character of Those Having R-Memories

The professional working with clients having R-memories of childhood incestuous abuse will encounter many who show the highly suggestible dissociative character dynamic which historically has been called "hysteria." The term derives from the Greek word for womb (as does "hysterectomy") and is applied far more often to women than to men. Because the word has sometimes been used in a way offensive to women, a different word might serve us better. Words are not easily replaced, however, especially when they refer to actualities in a unique and appropriate way. We could find no adequate substitute. See the Glossary for our description of the difference between popular, psychoanalytic, and Radix (our) use of the term. Here is how, as a Radix teacher, I understand the hysteric, or "dissociative-tending suggestible character structure" who produces R-memories.

On a body level, hysterics or those having hysteric tendencies combine an unusual aliveness in the pelvis with strong blocks and inhibitions in the upper body. The highly charged, alive pelvis requires strong blocking in the eyes, jaw, throat, chest, and diaphragm to contain the impulses the pelvis produces. If the upper body blocks don't overwhelm it, the free pelvis contributes to emotional aliveness, creativity and intelligence. People with this character dynamic are often emotionally expressive and other-oriented, and are commonly found in arts, music, drama, and dance. The active pelvis builds a charge that sometimes grows and overwhelms the upper body defenses. This usually results in the feeling that they are inadequate to deal with what they are. They are again and again swamped by feeling. They are often known for overdramatization, in which the feelings are escalated, made more of than is appropriate, "too much."

The highly charged pelvis of the hysteric-tending child fuels sexual feelings and fantasies. The sexual nature of these children may sometimes make them more subject to sexual abuse than are other children. This is not to suggest that they are at fault or in any way responsible for such abuse. A child is not responsible for having a precocious sexual nature. By the very nature of their character and development, these hysteric-tending children are trying to cope with feelings too powerful and grown up for them. They are unsure of themselves, look to and need help from others, and so easily become suggestible and vulnerable to influence.

Their perception of reality itself becomes subject to influence under the pressure of strong emotion and belief. They are more hypnotizable than other character structures, likely to accept ideas others would not, more influenced by relationship to others and less confident of their own ideas. This is true of child and adult alike.

Perhaps a few examples from literature and drama would help convey the nature of the hysteric character better than a general description:

Tennessee Williams' Maggie, in *Cat on a Hot Tin Roof*

Bizet's *Carmen*

Shakespeare's Kate in *The Taming of the Shrew*

Margaret Mitchell's Scarlett in *Gone with the Wind*

Jean Poiret's Albin in *La Cage Aux Folles*

Edward Albee's Martha, in *Who's Afraid of Virginia Woolf?*

I believe these examples illustrate the intense sexuality and escalated emotionality of the hysteric character. Poiret's Albin is the only male listed, and is perhaps the most prototypical hysteric in the group.

There are many times as many female as male hysterics. It is a genuine emotional/characterological difference between the sexes, rooted in a combination of biological and cultural factors. We won't try to sort out the nature and cause of these differences here. Just as male sexuality and emotionality is more frequently expressed aggressively than is women's, women's emotionality and sexuality is more frequently expressed through hysteria than is men's. Yet there are male hysterics, just as there are angry, aggressive women.

There is a "feminist/postmodernist" use of the term "male hysteric." The term is applied to exaggerated macho male sexuality.[62] Rambo, Terminator, and less physical figures of male power and authority personify this misuse of the term. But the term hysteria, whether male or female, should apply to escalated emotion and sexuality rather than exaggerated aggressiveness and power, granted that the two are related. Hysteria is something women and men do with their energy *instead* of expressing it in anger and power.

Freud spoke of hysteria as a "transference neurosis," in which the therapist has to analyze the relationship of client to therapist rather than the associations and character of the client per se. Relationship is supremely important to the hysteric because the self-concept is weak and the sexuality strong. Others are looked to, not just with sexual interest, but because hysterics rely on other people, on relationship, to help themselves develop a concept of self. This is also why they are so suggestible and subject to the influence of significant others.

Suggestions for Working with Clients Having R-Memories of Abuse

Hysteric, dissociative tending persons are prone to pseudomemories of incest, but they can also be abused as children. Their R-memories may therefore be authentic, be pseudomemories, or be some mixture of the two. Sex abuse issues should not be worked on in depth until progress has been made with dissociative elements of the hysteric structure, and until a real relationship of client to professional has been developed that can withstand stress. The work should follow the general principles previously outlined comparing regressive psychotherapy with the authors' approach to body work. In addition, here are a few more specific clinical suggestions appropriate to professionals able to use body work in their practice:

1) Work these people on their feet much of the time, eyes seeing and "in the room."

2) If they slip into emotional discharge to memory or fantasy events, slipping into discharge is the problem to be worked with, not the content of the events. Help them come back, gently at first, but insistently.

3) A defensive thought or image always has a body expression, formed by muscular tensions that inhibit or interfere with the life process. It is these tensions that the body worker focuses on, not the thoughts.

4) Keep them in an adult ego state as they work. As strong feelings come up they may tend to become overwrought, or to regress to a child-like upset voice, and pull back from eye contact. You want them to see you and speak to you adult to adult, "in the now."

5) Be easy and relaxed with them when possible, staying present and firm, a ready target for their anger when need be, a strong non-threatening presence when fear comes up, an empathizing friend when real pain arises, encouraging them to discharge feelings with awareness of the now, e.g., where they are and what they are doing.

6) The attention moves in and out between perception and memory or imagination. This is normal. Watch out when the stronger emotions are always tied to memory or imagination. This feeds the regressive tendency.

7) Vary the work to keep them with reality. When you feel them or yourself pulling back from eye contact yet they need more eye work, let them follow random movements of your penlight.[63] When they tire of being in serious adult conversation, but you're still fighting to keep them out of the regressed frightened or hurt child ego state, change the work. Kid them, ask them to sing, do body things, exercises, whatever you can do to keep them present.

8) First work with the eyes ("see me") then the eyes plus voice

("stay with me in the eyes and talk" or yell, sing, hum, or make other sounds).

9) When they really can't do an exercise because the defense is too strong, do the opposite, i.e., "go with the resistance," working for awareness of the block. Example: They *can't* yell out loud; the block is too strong—so have them listen *without self-reproach* to their over-soft, or whining or small voice, in session and out. In time, they'll discover and express with you the fear or anger or pain under the little voice, and the voice will open up.

10) Those with hysteric tendencies are uncentered in their life processes. Their attention goes out to their periphery and on out to the world, and doesn't want to come back in. They are self-conscious ("What do *you* think of me?") because they lack self-awareness ("Who am I? What do *I* think of me?"). Do centering work with them, and work with the poor self-concept that comes with lack of self-awareness and absence of connection to one's own being.

11) Although they are often highly talented and creative, their poor self-concept can undermine their ability to apply their talents. Help them to affirm their worth and to focus their energies.

12) Of course—stay with their breathing as you work. They will block against exhaling. Get the upper segments to open and the chest to drop at the same time, and they will be present and in good contact for a time.

13) Work regularly on transference issues. No character structure is more subject than theirs to transference distortion. Correcting transference distortion is central to their work. Those weak in self-awareness are over-aware of, and over-dependent on, significant others.

14) They may need psychotherapy as well as body work, especially

if they have serious dissociation problems. A body worker can team effectively with a therapist who understands and works in accord with the principles here. Let the therapist focus on the psychodynamics, while the body worker focusses on the body and character attitudes and with life processes in the body.

15) They may need medical interventions. Check things out with their physician. *They often have physical illnesses and symptoms.* Be careful when they are on psychoactive medication, e.g. tranquilizers, antidepressants, etc. or "recreational" drugs, including alcohol and marijuana. It is usually unwise to work with a student under the influence of psychoactive drugs, prescription or otherwise.

16) Watch for a "victim" character attitude in their work. The attitude is, "But how can I possibly be expected to live like an adult, be responsible for my own life, hold down a job, keep my appointments, pay my bills, try to form and nurture good human relationships? *I was abused,* you know." Unearth the attitude whenever it is expressed.

17) A group functioning on the principles listed here can be useful to them. Victim groups, groups encouraging regression, militant feminist, religious fundamentalist, or other ideology-focussed groups are apt to be harmful. (More will be said about this.)

18) Sometimes when they are present and in good contact, get them to talk about their abuse memories, adult to adult. Keep your own attitude non-judgmental. They may be dealing with memories or with pseudomemories, and which it is may have big ramifications for their life. You can't know. But at these times tell them about pseudomemories, their roots in vivid fantasy. They need to know that with R-memories there is always the possibility that even vivid, real-seeming memories are pseudomemories. And, their memories may be real. Encourage them to read this book if they haven't already.

19) Your job as a helping professional is to help them to become able to deal with their recovered memories of abuse thoughtfully and with feeling. The life decision as to whether the memories are real or are pseudomemories or a mix is, and must remain, theirs.

How *Not* to Deal With R-Memories

Therapy groups that contribute to the creation of R-memories of abuse are usually composed of a mix of people dealing with actual histories of incest and those having pseudomemories of incest. This helps further the fiction, believed by therapists and clients alike, that what they are dealing with is incest victims, when what they are dealing with is a mixture. Some of the clients are true incest victims, the great majority of whom have uninterrupted direct memory of the incest. Some of the clients are imaginary victims, however, the great majority of whom base their belief that they are incest victims on R-memories that are false or badly garbled; or they may believe they were incestuously abused but can't remember yet. Exposure to the group can feed into the development of pseudomemories:

> *When one group member would talk, it was sure to remind someone of something they were working on and bring out corresponding emotions. It was very upsetting for all to listen to the horrible and shocking stories of the women who had never forgotten their childhood molestation. It was heart-wrenching and emotionally draining. At times all of us would be crying and there was a box of tissues for us to pass around. My heart went out to these women. . . but I did not relate to their experiences.*
>
> *The women I related to were the ones trying desperately, like myself, to remember the repressed memories they had been diagnosed with, so they could heal. They too expressed doubts about the validity of the memories they had recovered during*

> *hypnotherapy and other treatments. They too felt angry at themselves for being in denial. They too were estranged from their extended family. They too were confused, frustrated, scared, and in tremendous emotional pain. They too were having trouble functioning in their day-to-day lives.*[64]

There will of course be a minority whose R-memories are genuine, who suffered actual traumatic amnesia.

The regressive techniques most influential in creating R-memories and fantasies of childhood often encourage a child-like state of consciousness in the client. *These techniques are usually bad for adults with real or imagined incest experiences in their lives.* If there is a real Post-Traumatic Stress Disorder tied to real incest experiences, talking about the experiences at an adult level with a sympathetic but not uncritical group of peers can be therapeutic. The group should be reality-oriented, focussed on real present-time functioning, accepting the ties this functioning has to a client's history. Groups which infantilize members at the first tears, use holding them, teddy bears, dolls, etc. for "comfort," undermine the real help that a group can otherwise be.

Evidence of bad incest therapy abounds. Some of the best-known therapists make extreme statements and advocate vengeful, ugly, and profoundly anti-therapeutic measures. These quotations are from *The Courage to Heal* by Ellen Bass and Laura Davis:[65]

> You may dream of murder or castration. It can be pleasurable to fantasize such scenes in vivid detail. . . . Let yourself imagine it to your heart's content. Giving yourself permission to visualize revenge can be satisfying indeed. (p. 128)

> There are nonviolent means of retribution you can seek. Suing your abuser and turning him in to the authorities are just two of the avenues open. (p. 128)

You may want to see them suffer. You may want revenge. ... You may want financial reparations or payment for your therapy. (p. 134)

Create an anger ritual (burn an effigy on the beach). ... Visualize punching and kicking the abuser when you do aerobics. (p. 129)

This woman probably would not have actually killed her father, but it felt good to think about it. (p. 143)

You are not more moral or courageous if you forgive. (p. 150)

Another woman, abused by her grandfather, went to his deathbed and, in front of all the other relatives, angrily confronted him right there in the hospital. (pp. 128-9)

Regarding this last statement, remember the man in a previous case who was abused sexually in his childhood by his teenage uncle, and who misremembered his grandfather as his abuser. Suppose he had gone storming into the hospital room when the innocent grandfather was on his deathbed with his family, to angrily confront him over sex abuse actually committed by someone else! Multiply by the thousands the false and garbled R-memories of incest produced by therapy practices across the country to begin to understand the magnitude of damage done by pseudotherapy based on producing R-memories.

There's a difference between allowing the safe spontaneous expression of anger and wreaking or imagining vengeance. Allowing the emergence of anger that has been blocked can be a freeing, empowering experience that integrates with one's life. Getting in touch with one's rage makes it easier to express appropriate anger in life. Often the ability to love will open up as well. Acting out of vengeance or visualizing violent revenge may give a temporary feeling of satisfaction but does not free the armor that blocks the underlying anger. The engendering of hatred and incitement to vengeance toward real or imagined abusers is seldom therapeutic, nor does it free victims from their blocked feelings. In cases of false memory, it distorts reality and damages or destroys important human relationships. It sets back the clients' therapy and their lives, even though it may sometimes make a victim feel better in the short term.

Yet there are some real cases of incest among those with R-memories. They may be relatively rare but they deserve respect and proper professional treatment. When there is substantial solid evidence of incestuous sex abuse, confrontation of one's abuser may sometimes help the victim deal with what happened. Exposure and legal action may at times be in order. The purpose should not be revenge or retribution, but to protect other potential victims from the abuser, to set a false record straight, or other justifiable motives. When there is no corroborative evidence, talking with the remembered abuser and/or other family members may help the client sort out his or her feelings and learn what, if anything, actually happened.

It is not always wise to group clients working on incest problems together. Group members who are deeply depressed and/or over-emotional can feed into each others' emotions. It can deepen the problem if they express their feelings without a strong guide to help them work through their troubled feeling states. The consequences can be severe:

> *In group we regularly talked about explicit sexual abuse in a small room while screaming, yelling details, and beating things with bats. You hear this for an hour and a half every day and sometimes an hour at night, and you get to where you really don't know what went on in your life. We also talked specifically about what we did to harm ourselves. I used a very dan-*

gerous substance that induces vomiting and I had to talk about my use of this. One woman went home and tried what she had heard me describe and she died.[66]

Treating Pseudomemories as Truth

If pseudomemories are treated as authentic in life as well as in therapy sessions, the life of the client as well as the progress of the work will degenerate into chaos. Unquestioned pseudomemories require that a pseudoreality be created to match. Innocent family members are treated as sex criminals. Others are expected by the client to accept these false memories as reality and may be cut out of the client's life if they do not. Family relationships are destroyed, and real progress in therapy becomes impossible, because client and professional have accepted and try to pursue the pseudoreality.

The client suspected of having pseudomemories should not be told that the memories are false, but should be told of the widespread existence of pseudomemories, and that his or her R-memories *may or may not be true*. It is important to leave the judgment to the client.—And the client needs to stop working regressively. If they work regressively the pseudoreality will grow, involving new instances of abuse, perhaps new "perpetrators." The abuses in pseudomemory will become more extreme and dramatic, the pseudoreality they occur in less credible. Intimates are expected to believe and to support the increasingly crazy pseudoreality, or become alienated. The unfortunate client loses ground. Assured that progress is being made, the client gets worse. If there is a dissociative disorder, it intensifies. If there are multiple personalities more are developed. The client slips into regressive states more easily, produces more intense pseudomemories, and copes with real life less effectively. This downhill slide can go on for years with no real end in sight. The stories of retractors in Chapter Three speak to

DEALING WITH MEMORIES OF INCESTUOUS ABUSE 83

this point. Pseudomemories tend to proliferate, becoming more bizarre, involving more people, stretching over larger spans of time. A mother of an accuser wrote:

> *Her sisters started doubting her sexual abuse accusations after she also accused her father of murdering a hitchhiker in our basement and he and I of burying him in the backyard . . . the list* [of accusations] *kept growing and continuing to an older and older age . . .* [until] *the sexual molestation had allegedly gone on until she was eighteen. These were all said to be "repressed memories."*[67]

Real memories are limited, then, confined as they are by the facts of reality, but pseudomemories are apt to keep expanding. This can be a means of differentiating pseudomemories from real memories. Another letter by an accused father:

> *Briefly, our thirty-two-year old daughter has falsely accused first me, then my wife, then my mother, and now my father (who is eighty-seven years old) of sexual and satanic ritual abuse.*[68]

And finally, a quote from an article in the *Houston Chronicle* of September 12, 1993:

> *Lucy Abney went into treatment for depression but came out with more than 100 alternate personalities and horrifying memories of a past spent in a satanic cult. By the time Abney finished two years of therapy, she had flashbacks of cannibalism, blood drinking, orgies, and the sacrifice of three of her babies. She said her therapist warned that some of her personalities could be turned on or off by a secret "programming code" and that her husband was a high priest in the satanic cult.*
>
> *"The memories were real, very vivid," said Abney, who said she had never had such visions before she began therapy in 1991. But after leaving a psychiatric hospital where she had*

spent nearly a year and more than $300,000, Abney suddenly had doubts about her bizarre memories: Were they real or fantasy? Abney, 45, of Houston decided they were fantasy and she blames her psychologist for her false memories and misplaced concerns about satanism.[69]

The retractor items describe the lucky ones. They have finally recognized their pseudomemories for what they are, and have given up the pseudoreality that cost them so dearly. Now they are back in reality, and begin the job of rebuilding their lives. They can try to reestablish relationships with family members they had falsely accused, recover financially from the drain of years of bad therapy, find organizations and activities where they are more than a patient and pseudovictim. At last they are dealing appropriately with their pseudomemories of abuse.

The unlucky others continue to maintain a pseudoreality of incest and abuse. They must continue, cling to, and pay for a therapy that makes them worse and the activities it provides to substitute for the family they abandoned. There they are in their incest "survivors" group, the pseudovictims mixed with real incest victims who are moving ahead with their lives as they learn to deal with the real incidents of incest they went through. For those harboring pseudomemories instead, the ever-growing pseudomemories define an ever changing pseudoreality to which they attach their downwardly spiraling lives. When people live in unreality their futures are bleak, and their unreality can do irreparable damage, not only to their own lives but to the lives of significant others:

> *I confronted my mother. She told me that she had nothing more to live for, and she drove her car off a bridge. She is dead. Now I'm not sure about the memories.*[70]

So it may go with people who try to live on the basis of pseudomemories of abuse.

6

Commentary

This book was developed from a series of articles on recovered memories of incestuous abuse in *Chuck Kelley's Radix Newsletter*, issues 13, 14, and 15. Reader interest has been lively, and comments and questions from readers have played their part throughout the preceding chapters. Responses are still coming in, informed, articulate, thoughtful responses, in the form of the kind of dialog with its readers that the *Newsletter* has sought to develop. The responses broaden our viewpoint, add to our understanding, and here contribute to this book. We thank every correspondent, even when, and sometimes especially when, they disagree with what we have said. We invite present readers to continue the process.[71]

A European therapist writes:

I must tell you that your attitude towards "recovered memories" of sexual abuse disturbs me. I think that a healthy skepticism is different than judging what is and what is not "confabulation." You are judging the memories of others' experiences—of events where you were <u>not</u> present! I believe that the consequences of judging an accurate memory as "confabulated" is just as, if not more, dangerous and damaging than judging a "confabulated" memory as true.

Most sexual (and physical) abuse takes place in secrecy—often without the knowledge of anyone but abuser and victim—and often the victim is threatened if s/he ever tells anyone—sometimes with death.

Even if the victim is not threatened, s/he usually has so much guilt about the abuse that s/he is afraid to tell anyone. Often the victim is told that it is his/her fault that the abuser does what s/he does. The father that accuses the daughter of her sexiness, the mother that accuses her son that his behavior forces her to violence. A vulnerable kid, dependent on his/her parents, is likely to believe what s/he is told, if only to try to make sense out of what is happening.

There are almost never records of evidence. What 3-year-old has the wherewithal to go to the police and say, "my father raped me, take me to a doctor for a pelvic exam?" What 5-year-old, told that if she ever tells she'll be killed, will dare to even whisper it.

Dissociation is a major feature of all trauma, including sexual abuse. The degree varies from person to person and trauma to trauma. It can be as severe as complete amnesia, conversion hysteria or multiple personality, but is usually less so—forgotten event, partially remembered event, blocked or discounted emotions, dissociated body symptoms (numbness in hands, sexual deadness), and any combination or degree of these. Therefore: A MAJOR SYMPTOM OF SEXUAL ABUSE IS THAT IT IS <u>NOT</u> REMEMBERED!!!

Of course, dissociation makes the work of the therapist harder, both in helping the victim to work through the trauma, and in helping the victim to find out the reality in it. My point is that you close doors to that with your attitude of judging "confabulation." I believe your attitude could be damaging to an already self-doubting sexual abuse victim. <u>It is the victim who must come to terms with his/her reality, not you!</u>

The author, an American body-oriented psychotherapist now practicing in Europe, is trained as a clinical social worker, as a Radix teacher, and as a practitioner of Lillemor Johnsen's form of body work.

COMMENTARY

Chuck Kelley responds:

Your letter was written in response to only part one of my *Newsletter* series on recovered memories. I expect your alarm would have been reduced with a fuller picture of my viewpoint. Frankly, I do have a healthy skepticism about particular R-memories, recognizing from the start that some are true, some false, and some garbled. Yes, I do judge them if I consider it appropriate to do so. For example, I judge the R-memories of Michelle in *Michelle Remembers* to be false, as I do almost all other R-memories of satanic ritual abuse and of alien abduction. I could be wrong. I read their stories, but am not convinced. R-memories of incestuous abuse are harder to judge, because such abuse is rather common, and may be masked by some of the factors you describe. The appropriate stance is usually not to judge, but to educate the client to understand that his/her R-memories may or may not be literally true. Since I know that some R-memories of abuse are true, and that false ones have a psychological significance, I listen to the stories with respect, but encourage restraint about acting on them.

I confess that the rest of your letter contains too much victimology for me. Yes, incest is terrible and innocent children suffer from it. Innocent clients and families victimized by pseudo-memories of incest created in therapy also suffer, as retractor testimonies show. The point is to try to get to the truth of things. Corroborative evidence can be found in some cases—abuser confessions, diaries, other family members' continuous memories. No, most incest does not create traumatic amnesia, and most incest victims remember the experience clearly. No, it is not true that "A MAJOR SYMPTOM OF SEXUAL ABUSE IS THAT IT IS *NOT* REMEMBERED." It is a silly assertion, since it is clear that "not remembering" sexual abuse is equally "symptomatic" of not having been sexually abused. And I think that helping a client "work through the traumas" embodied in false R-memories is profoundly antitherapeutic. On the last sentence of your letter at least, we mostly agree. Yes it is the client who must come to terms with his/her reality, as I have made clear.—Only you say the *victim* must come to terms, indicating your own tendency to prejudge the truth of an R-memory.

Roger Wescott writes:

It's interesting, I think, that all three types of remembered abuse [satanic ritual abuse, alien abductions, and sexual abuse -ed.] *involve sexual manipulation. This seems to give further validation to both Freud and Reich.*

To repeat what I wrote to you earlier: "I believe that, just as we can have other people's dreams, we can have other people's memories. What A recalls as having happened to herself may actually have happened— but to B." (This may be true even when A does not know B.)

Among fantasized memories of purely sexual abuse, one of the most common types, I would guess, is in situations, such as erotic feeling shared by father and daughter, where an intense attraction is mis-remembered as overt behavior. This too is classically Freudian.

As regards satanic ritual abuse, the key word may not be satanic (since the gods of one context can be the demons of another) but ritual. There is, I believe, at least minimal pathology inherent in every rite and every institution—spontaneously felt, I think, by children. As a child, I myself for example felt as oppressed and coerced by weddings as by funerals: all such observances seemed alien to me.

Dr. Roger Wescott, Emeritus Professor of Anthropology of Drew University, is a cultural anthropologist and psychohistorian. His contributions relating to Reichian and Radix theory span a period of more than thirty years.

Chuck Kelley responds:

You make the startling suggestion that we may at times have other people's memories, so that R-memories may be of other people's experience. It's an intriguing thought, but as a wide-ranging psychologist, I just have never seen any evidence for such a transfer of conscious experience from one mind to another and, until I do, I remain wedded to the idea that memories are dependent on traces in an individual's nervous system. Your well-taken point about R-memories of father-daughter incest is virtually the same as we wrote (quite independently) in Chapter Five, and is classically Freudian, as you say. I'm glad we agree. That and your initial observation about the role of sex in all three types of abuse do support Freud and Reich on sexuality.

Your paragraph about the pathology in every ritual, not just those of satanic ritual abuse, also intrigued me. Like you, I felt oppressed as a child by the simple rituals in my fundamentalist Christian upbringing. These were for me prayers at table and bedtime, communion, christenings and baptisms at church, people "giving their lives to Christ" in meetings, prayers for divine intervention on earth, etc. Magic as a game is fun, but ritual magic taken seriously is irrational. It is terrifying to a child to face being in a situation where lunatics run the asylum he is trapped in. Yet there are certain observances, ceremonies—rituals, if you will—that I see as significant and of value. I include a moment's silence before a family meal together, a birthday cake with candles and gifts to celebrate, a graduation with caps and gowns, a memorial service for one who has died. When do happy and useful ceremonies become an oppressive and irrational ritual? Is it when the ceremony is accorded supernatural significance?

Judith Searle writes:

The Radix Newsletter with Part 3 of "Recovery of Repressed Memories" arrived today, and I read it all with great interest (as I did the first two parts)....

I suppose part of the reason I didn't set fingers to computer keyboard about the first two parts of your excellent piece is that I felt it all made such evident good sense, I couldn't believe anyone would take issue with what you'd written. Part 3 is equally strong. . . .

I'm not a therapist myself, and my only experience of anything like therapy has been personal Radix work with two superb teachers who have become treasured friends. However, I have heard enough horror stories from friends and relatives to feel that therapists have probably been responsible for more mental health problems and psychic pain than has any other single factor in our society.

I think the basic problem arises from American society being so hung up on science and technology that it has historically been unable to distinguish between the pseudoscience of psychology and "hard" sciences. The fact that psychologists, marriage and family therapists, and social workers all refer to what they do as "science" (and have professional organizations dedicated to promulgating that fiction) has successfully pulled the wool over the eyes of the health insurance industry so that the "health care" these sometimes helpful, sometimes dangerous folk offer has been mindlessly accorded the same status as treatments for heart attacks, diabetes, and cancer. This does not, to my mind, change the reality that psychotherapy is, at best, a craft (I believe Radix work, for instance, is a finely-honed craft worthy of respect) and, at worst, a fraud on the public.

It is said that every nation gets the government it deserves, and it might also be said that we get the therapy we deserve. America has historically been so hung up about sexuality, so Puritanical (in the worst sense of the word) that it is a joke in Europe and throughout much of the rest of the world. Reich suffered much because of his writing and working to challenge some of the sexual prissiness of this country, and the same forces that brought him down are still at work (certainly in the religious right).

The books purporting to catalogue the horrors of satanic abuse and other sexual horrors have in the past few years become a particularly insidious form of pornography, in my view, and their distribution serves to increase the hysteria and confabulation, much as the news of the Salem witch-burnings fed on itself and produced new reports of ever more heinous atrocities from suggestible and hysterical people. Those who are discontented with their lives can easily be led to see themselves as victims of some evil "out there," be it sexual abuse by family members, satanic cult adherents, or aliens from outer space.

My own view is that television, by replacing family interactions with a kind of shared social trance, has made people's vulnerability to dredging up confabulated memories (with the "help" of self-deluded therapists) greater now than it was thirty years ago. It is harder for children now to separate fact from fiction on television (with all the "docu-dramas" and dramas "based on a true story" currently on the tube, it's getting harder for adults, too).

Fortunately, a few respected publications have recently begun to question the current witch hunt. Carol Tavris's article in the New York Times Book Review *in January, 1993, expressing her objections to the plethora of books by the Davis/Bass/Fredrickson contingent, was an important opening wedge. So also was the two-part article earlier this year in the* New Yorker *about the satanic abuse trial in the Northwest. Your own excellent articles make another strong contribution.*

Judith Searle, a writer, editor, and actress, heads the West Coast Division of the Editorial Department, a professional editing organization.

Chuck Kelley responds:

You lay it to the psychotherapists as being responsible for more mental health problems and psychic pain than any other single factor in our society. I myself would still accord that distinction to fundamentalist religion, with compulsory state education a close second, but R-memories are primarily associated with psychotherapy. I agree that psychology is not a science. The problem is specifically that psychotherapy deals with metaphorical diseases based on a medical analogy, as Thomas Szasz has made so clear.[72] People with chronic anxieties, stresses, unhappiness, moral difficulties, problems with relationships—the psychotherapists' stock in trade—are given an artificial, often inappropriate set of labels, modeled after medical disease categories. Thus people who have, or with help develop, R-memories of incestuous or satanic ritual abuse may be diagnosed as suffering from Post-Traumatic Stress Disorder, Conversion Disorder, Multiple Personality Disorder, or other of the psychiatric classifications which allow reimbursement from health insurance plans. When the disorder is produced in the service of the diagnosis, fraud is too kind a word for it.

Psychotherapy itself is receiving a well-deserved black eye over the R-memories issue, but caution is in order. Important techniques for changing people's character and lives have been developed and are being practiced under the label of psychotherapy. Freud, Reich, Perls, Berne, and I would add Bar-Levav, physicians all, developed such techniques, thinking they were developing medical treatment procedures. But non-physicians, F. M. Alexander, Ida Rolf, Moishe Feldenkrais, Werner Erhardt, Dale Carnegie, Carl Rogers, and Krishnamurti, to name but a few, contributed other kinds of techniques. Radix is my own contribution in this direction. Our need is to get out from under the burden of the medical model, learn to sift the wheat from the chaff of these many and varied processes, and move ahead on developing new forms of education, the aim of which is growth in the whole person, physically, emotionally, morally, socially. But I'm getting a little off my point, which is that good psychotherapists have a craft of great value, and do wonderful things with and for people coming to them. The error is to consider them as therapists engaged in treating medical illness when they are really teachers of a different kind than the educational system produces.

I agree with the substance of what you say about television and the "shared social trance." Kids (and adults) need interaction with intelligent conscious people to discover who they are and create who they will become. Those most subject to suggestion — the hysterics — have the least concept of who they are and are most bewildered by their sexuality. They are the ones most prone to fashion fads, cult religions and pseudomemories of all kinds.

We're glad to have your references concerning confabulated memories.

Alice Ladas writes:

Many people are now giving serious thought to the problem of memory as it pertains to abuse.

R. has been a client off and on since her late teenage years. Child of a psychotic abusive mother and a brilliant, passive father, she was angry, dysfunctional, and literally smelled bad. During the first years of therapy, she became able to finish school and begin to support herself marginally. After a hiatus, she returned, got a graduate degree, reverted to her religious origins, and married. After another hiatus, she returned to therapy. Now she has children and a good job, but is still sexually frozen. Although we knew about the abuses to which she had been subjected and had worked with them on a body level, she was never able to fully come into her body until I worked with her lips and mouth, using a technique I learned in a workshop for helping dysfunctional animals with Linda Tellington-Jones. R. is now beginning to really feel her body, and the abuse from her mother and later at school where she was gang raped is becoming real to her, not just intellectually. Her whole self is beginning to unravel and reintegrate. Memories in three dimensions are returning. One eye and her frozen legs have been key aspects of her bodily blocks that are now changing. The real key to her frozenness was not the abuse itself, but the fact that her parents, learning about the gang rape at school, sent her back to that school, ignoring her request that they not discuss the problem with the school directors. As a result, she was thrown back into an even more threatening environment, having been betrayed by her parents. The betrayal was worse than the abuse itself. What we are dealing with now is her ambivalence about trusting anyone, her husband and myself especially since we are the closest. As she deals with this, her body is softening and she is beginning to feel sexual pleasure for the first time.

Dr. Alice Ladas, a bioenergetic therapist and sexologist, helped found the Institute for Bioenergetic Analysis. She has been my research partner in the study of sexuality and we have co-led workshops in sexual enhancement. She is the first author of the best-selling book *The G-Spot*.

Chuck Kelley responds:

I've included your letter because it illustrates how a good body-oriented psychotherapist deals with an extremely traumatized, sexually frozen person. I hope she hangs in with you now that you have worked in and down with her to the deep pelvic material.

Reuven Bar-Levav writes:

Your article on the "Recovery of Repressed Memories, Part Three" and on pseudomemories is thorough and excellent. It addresses a very serious and not widely enough recognized problem which causes a great deal of damage to lots of people, already in distress. . . . Here are a couple of points whose focus deserves to be sharpened a little more:

When false memories are being treated as true the main danger is not that this can lead to "false accusations against innocents," although this also happens. Much worse, it makes room for a permanent status of victim that henceforth justifies the making of claims on others. This widespread tendency is now creating a new class of embittered cripples, people who are condemned to live on handouts without the pride of eating the fruits of their own labor. The status of victim entitles its holder to live regressively at least until full compensation for alleged past suffering has been paid. Philosophically and practically it overemphasizes the rights of our citizens and neglects our obligations, thus weakening the social fiber. This all fits well with what you said in describing the attitude of the "victim" character (in number sixteen [page 77] of your numbered clinical suggestions).

Everyone who works with people should read and reread this point that you make so succinctly. Those millions who now self-righteously subscribe to such an attitude are indeed victimized by it, regardless of how much or how little they also suffered in the past. The victim status is immensely harmful to everyone but the lawyers who try to establish it and as you point out, "have everything to gain from a successful suit." Those defined as victims have a stake in continuing to see themselves as abused, and others as abusers. This becomes their life-long self-image. It also condemns such victims to never having decent and trusting relationships with anyone else, except with others who carry a similar grudge.

I am not sure that you are right about the intermediaries being "virtually all. . . sincere." I believe you are too generous in this regard, which is dangerous. More often than not, the intermediaries are also zealots with the same pathological values as those they claim to represent. In fact they are often the ones who throw oil into the fire and make the conflagration of hate much worse.

In a sense, everyone without exception has been an abused child. We must all live for well over a year in total or almost total isolation before we become conscious of externality and of others. This is what "normal autism" is all about. We are all born prematurely in a psychologic sense, without any understanding of anything. We all have a seemingly endless number of experiences that subjectively are most terrifying, as I have described fully in my writings.[73] *Before we are even aware of the terrible fears of abandonment and engulfment, the faceless fear of Non-Being has already tortured every one of us a thousand times. The pseudomemories of child abuse, satanic ritual abuse or alien abduction all have a face, and by giving it a comprehensible meaning they thus lessen the continuing inner threat of that most horrible of all fears. This is the source of the confusion. In discussing this fear I describe the more innocent fascination with science-fiction which also serves the same purpose, but without crippling those who use it.*

There is only one point with which I must take issue, but I suspect that here too we agree as you reflect upon it. . . . In writing about the survey of clinical psychologists from the American Psychological Association on the frequency of satanic ritual abuse patients in their practices since 1980, you report that:

> *Seventy percent of the respondents had seen no such cases at all. The majority of the remaining thirty percent had seen one case. . . . However, sixteen psychologists, comprising six tenths of one percent of the 2,709 respondents, reported seeing one hundred or more, up to two thousand religious abuse cases, most of them involving satanism.*

Your conclusion that these sixteen psychologists are the ones who "are specializing in the area" is, in my opinion, out and out wrong. Much more likely, these psychologists fit better into your earlier description:

> *Pseudomemories become a widespread group phenomenon when they are seized on by the zealots of a popular belief system and used for evidence of the validity of that system.*

Therapists who repeatedly express their bias by asking highly suggestible people about how they were abused, are eventually likely to get confirmation from frightened individuals who wish to please those who have some power over them. This is a tragic if not a callous phenomenon. You have described it clearly and well.

All in all I want to compliment you on having made this contribution. . . . More power to you and I hope that this important discussion reaches the widest possible audience.

Dr. Reuven Bar-Levav is a Detroit psychiatrist, founder of Crisis Mobilization Therapy and of the Bar-Levav Educational Association, a major post-graduate training organization for psychotherapists in the Midwest. He has just completed a second book, on fathering.

Chuck Kelley responds:

You are a case in the point I just made to Judith Searle. You are one of the most powerful, effective teachers of personal growth that I know, though you steadfastly insist that you are a psychotherapist doing medical work. Your letter is a good example of your clarity of thinking and directness of expression. There is little I can take issue with. Your emphasis on the victim psychology of those with R-memories of incest is to the point, and carries the matter further than did we.

A word about your comment concerning the study ascertaining that most of the work with satanic ritual abuse clients is done by a fraction of one percent of the 2,700 psychologists surveyed. We endeavored to withhold judgment regarding the work done by these psychotherapists working with SRA cases. I know that many of them are religious zealots and modern day witch hunters, but I hope that *some* are clear-headed, rational, and able to help their clients come to terms with reality rather than lose themselves in R-memories of questionable authenticity.

We have some disagreement regarding developmental theory. I agree that there is a sense in which "we are all abused children," but I don't tie it to infantile "fears of non-being." I am much more of a Freudian than you, and have found no general framework that fits my experience of early childhood better than the Freudian framework embracing infantile sexuality, id, ego, and superego. Like Dr. Wescott, I see evidence of Freudian and Reichian sexuality everywhere—including this R-memories work.

Ralphine Cierpial writes:

The article is an excellent presentation of the subject. Broad in scope and principled, this work is instructive and educational. The last of your nineteen clinical suggestions is the best of all.

I question working with body parts, e.g., the eyes. My personal experiences with eye work are usually dissociative. The defense is in small part ocular or psychological and often requires the muscles and some body actions to release and to integrate feeling processes.

Ralphine Cierpial is a Radix teacher, not currently in practice, and a long-time friend of Radix work.

Chuck Kelley responds:

Thank you for the kind words. I'm interested in your point about work with the eyes being dissociative in your experience. In general, I have found eye work integrative and sane-making. So many people go "off" in the eyes, and good eye work brings them back. I have noticed sometimes, however, that penlight work can feed a split between the ocular and oral segments of the body, which means, as you know, the two major systems of thinking: visual thinking, and inner speech. The split between them is an important dissociation. It calls for ocular-oral integration and, ultimately, integration with the other body segments, as you state. That's how I understand your remarks about eye work and dissociation.

But regressive memories and fantasies, so important in the hysteric character structure, become vivid and compelling when visual perception of real persons and surroundings is shut down. R-memories and fantasies are driven by the oral segment, by verbal thought, rooted bodily in implicit speech. The problem then is to get awareness through the eyes, which are not a small part, but a major part of the defenses. After the eyes perceive and the thought processes engage what is in front of the eyes, the thought processes can expand to embrace a larger view of reality. What is present and real to the senses provides the hub, the central system of reference for the wheel of reality. There lies the importance of the ocular segment.

Ellen Baker writes:

I have been following with interest your Newsletter *articles on recovered memories. Sexual and physical abuse is common in our Patriarchal culture, but is still a "taboo" socially, so the abused child must find a way to survive in a family where abuse is really happening, but everyone acts as if it is not. Before boundaries are fully formed, the child can adapt by believing the family is sane and he is crazy or by repressing his memory and pretending the family is fine. I suspect abuse of older children is more readily remembered than that of younger children who may be more likely to suppress. Radix seems to be very effective in opening blocks in the body that allow repressed memory to be recalled. It seems not unusual that we would find such students with low self-image, often feeling like victims. I agree that the goal with any student, including abuse cases, is to work through the victim posture and encourage the adult ego state. I appreciate the distinction that real memories have definition and limited scope while pseudomemories grow in a web of confusion, because that is also my experience. . . .*

I see your guidelines as significant and appropriate for working with regressive memories. However, I do take issue with part of what you say about regression. While it is important to keep people in contact and not to relate to them from their regressed perspective, I find it is valuable to accept students as they deepen into regressive memory because in that state they actually feel how it was to BE that child in that event. Having contacted deep old emotions, many students are then able to discharge more fully and integrate more deeply in the adult state. So, I disagree with you about NEVER letting students regress. It may happen because it needs to, and the teacher should not stop the student unless there is a history of splitting or uncontrolled behavior. I believe the crux of the matter here is the state of consciousness present in regression. I see it as BEING the child again, in which the adult state is not present, but the observing ego is. On request, regressed students come back to adult awareness. This is even true of those who regress to infantile states as soon as they become overcharged. These softer structures do not re-

quire much charging to get into strong feelings, and it takes conscious effort for them not to slip into regression. The rigid structures have to work to get deeply enough into feeling to regress and are more able to remain on the "edge," though it still requires purpose. I suspect there are inherent differences in how anger blockers and fear blockers (in your Radix characterology) regress on the basis of their structures. It may be easier for an anger type to come out or stay out of regression due to their outward flow and peripheral charge capacity. It might be easier for a fear type to slip in and harder to come out, given their inward flow direction. In any event, it does require purpose to remain in deep feeling with enough observing ego to correlate past and present. Reaching that balance requires that the teacher be able to see when the student is present, allow regressive experience, and gently bring the student back. If the teacher disallows regression, the student may feel "wrong" and will likely either project negatively or pull back from interaction. On the other hand, if the teacher promotes regression, with no focus on developing awareness in the present, the student will likely go through many sessions without significant progress and may remain a victim of the event, forever reliving it instead of moving on. . . .

I believe memories recovered USING regressive techniques are different than regressive states arising spontaneously. The former is more prone to confabulation, given the unspoken expectation that something is to be "found out." Spontaneous recovery of memory often occurs when a student feels safe enough to allow recall, often after doing considerable Radix work. As an example, I worked with a female student in her forties with four years of Radix experience, in the area of sexuality. She experienced a repressed memory from age four while exploring her own sexuality. The entire memory took about four weeks to unfold, though most of it was revealed in one evening following a good sexual release with her partner. The memory was present with sight, sound, and smells and textures of the original event, but she was unable to see the face of the abuser, despite a strong conscious desire to know. The memory continued without significant change for four weeks, until she had almost *given up knowing who it was. Following another strong sexual release, she saw clearly the face of the abuser. She could have "assumed" it was her father or any other man, but it was very important to wait until full awareness came to recall. I agree with you on the importance of not escalating unclear memories and of not digging for identities. It is equally important to accept what is recovered and to check into reality for supporting evidence. This student checked what she could with living relatives, and found nothing inconsistent with her recovered memory. Of course, forty years is a long time. The offender is dead now and cannot be confronted directly, but her work in releasing the fear and rage has continued, and she is progressing well in her work at this time.*

Let me say again that I do recognize the damage that can follow when confabulated memories are taken as real. I know a poignant case of a father who recently lost visitation with his children on the basis of confabulated memories occurring in his ex-wife's therapy. . . .

One last point about the hysteric structure you often describe as being dramatic, escalating feeling, exaggerating emotion, having a precocious fascination with sexuality, and a high level of suggestibility. I recognize these traits in some of my students in varying degrees. I also recognize that repressed memories are prone to contamination in the unconscious, so they must be deciphered carefully and rationally. I agree that feelings are often polarized around a single event, when in fact they represent a larger group of events of a certain type. But even given all this, a young child is open and trusting until he learns not to be. Subjected to sexual abuse at an early age, he learns some terrifying lessons. He has no rational frame of reference in which to express his feelings and integrate his experience unless he is lucky enough to be found and comforted by a loving adult. Is it any wonder that his behavior becomes dramatic, escalated, exaggerated, sexually oriented, and highly suggestible? Early abuse of any kind surely enhances, and may even instill, hysteric character traits, and a child's best defense and hope for survival may well be repression of the memory until he is safe and secure enough to recall and deal with it.

In summary, I propose that the most effective way to work with regressive memory is to develop in the student a balance of deep feeling capacity with a competent, rational adult state. I believe that awareness of present time and space does form a bridge for integrating feelings of the past into the present. I also feel that regressed memory may be a genuine repository for blocked feeling, and can become a valuable connection with deeper processes that need release. As always, the balance between feeling and purpose is crucial in understanding our experiences.

Ellen Baker is Co-director, with her husband, of the Kentucky Center for Experiential Education. Her qualifications include a year of training in Kelley/Radix work under my direction.

Chuck Kelley responds:

Your long, thoughtful letter agrees with most but takes issue with a few of the points that we have made. A major point of issue is regression, and when or if to allow a client tending to regress to do so. I am firm in teaching professionals studying with me to keep an extremely tight rein on regression in their clients. I don't think that in a regressed state clients ". . . actually feel how it was to *BE* that child in that event," or that they recreate "the sights, sounds, and textures of the original event." In my experience, clear vivid detailed regressive memories and fantasies often are strikingly different from actual events, and usually reflect a process more like dreamwork than authentic memory. It is a serious error to assume R-memories are true because they are clear and vivid. Several of our retractors learned this to their sorrow.

Many people become addicted to playing exciting regressive fantasies to themselves as a substitute for facing the prosaic but real requirements of their lives. Sometimes I do deliberately encourage regressive fantasies in Radix clients, often in showing them the difference between fantasy and reality, and rehearsing them on how to lift out of fantasy and return to reality fully and quickly. More rarely I do it to help a client learn to use fantasy and imagination when this is difficult for him. I don't agree that people can maintain an observing ego when they give up their adult ego state in the service of regression. The observing ego *is* adult real-time consciousness. And I don't agree that "regressed memory may be a genuine repository for blocked feeling." The muscular armor is the means by which feelings are blocked, not the "regressed memory." Release of the armor frees the feelings, and may trigger old memories, but sinking regressively into old memories is *not* a good approach to freeing the armor which blocks the feelings. People can do it for years and make no significant progress. As a technique of therapy it is seductive, indulgent, and ultimately dangerous to those with hysteric tendencies, and therefore to therapists and Radix teachers who use it in their practices. This is not an exaggeration, and I speak from experience, not theory.

Another point from your letter. You state that "sexual and physical abuse are common in our Patriarchal culture." The reference to patriarchal culture here is gratuitous feminist cant. Incestuous child abuse occurs most often in families which lack a strong, present father. In our examples, Shirley had no father in her mother-ruled home, and was abused by her mother's father. Martha was raped, not by her father, but by her mother's scummy second husband. — And remember the mother who enticed men home from bars by promising them sexual access to her daughter in their fatherless home, and the mother living alone with her son who showed her "mama's boy" son how to masturbate. In my experience, Jews and Mormons and others having strong stable patriarchal family structures tend to have low incidences of incest, while children in loose father-absent or weak family structures are vulnerable to abuse by male relatives and other males brought into the home by mothers. Of course there are good mother-ruled families but they require an especially strong woman, one able to be both mother and father to the children.

Your argument about sexual abuse instilling hysteric character traits in a child could be used to "explain" almost any character syndrome, e.g., "Is it any wonder that the abused child's behavior becomes withdrawn, reclusive, emotionally flat, and lacking in affect"—or whatever other set of symptoms one wishes to "explain" as being due to incestuous abuse.

As to your closing suggestion concerning the "most effective way to work with regressive memory," I maintain that the most effective way is *not* to work with regressive memory, but to work with the character structure of those who make use of our skills. This is because I have seen Radix teachers come to grief on this issue again and again, and I caution you specifically about it. It is the persistent tying of their strongest emotions to events created in fantasy or reminiscence rather than to real people and here-and-now events that nourishes regressive tendencies at the expense of real life. Because they are tied to the strongest emotion, these fantasies draw the attention until life becomes organized around them. This is how they lead in the direction of withdrawal from reality. And yes, as you say, a central objective of good Radix work is attainment of a balance of deep feeling capacity with a competent rational adult state. In that we do agree.

I'm sorry if I have sometimes slipped back into my teacher-to-student role in this reply. It's a little like not always seeing my grown children as full-fledged adults. I hope that nevertheless what I've said is useful in your Radix practice.

7

Conclusion

Many R-memories of childhood incest develop by a process of fantasy rather than through recall of the facts of reality. These are *pseudomemories*, the false memories Freud discovered in regressing hysteric clients to explore their early history. Freud reported this work early in this century. The incest fantasies may appear clearly, and in detail. Therapists using regressive techniques have rediscovered Freud's techniques, using them to create vivid incest fantasies in their clients, and treating them as true memories. By encouraging clients to act on the basis of these false memories, they have created great disruptions and stress in family relationships. Retractors who have described their therapy have remarked on how vivid the fantasy scenes were, even when they were aware they were making the material up. R-memories of satanic ritual abuse and of abduction and abuse aboard alien spacecraft reflect the same kind of fantasy process. These R-memories illustrate pseudomemories that masquerade as truth.

R-memories cannot all be dismissed as fantasy, for they often have real elements, major or minor. These elements may be distorted or shifted to make a garbled memory, one that is false in certain essential features, but is not fantasy. Consider the man who developed R-memories of being abused sexually as a child by his grandfather when the abuser was not the grandfather at all but was instead an uncle, who acknowledged what he had done. Remember "Laurel" and her intense sex games as a young child with playmate Jay Rubin, our correspondent. Decades later, Laurel developed R-memories of these games in therapy, but misremembered her partner as her older brother rather than her playmate. Thus she converted her innocent childhood sex play into guilty incestuous perversity, accusing the evidently guiltless brother to others in their family. Then there was the woman who had R-memories of incestuous abuse at the hand of an uncle, but her uncle proved to be off fighting the Korean war at the time the alleged abuse took place, and she decided it must have been her father. Consider yet another woman's R-memories of childhood incestuous abuse by her father in the attic of a home in which it seems there was no attic.

Garbled R-memories of abuse include elements of truth. There often was sexual abuse somewhere at some time by someone, but the facts are obscure, the memories plastic, the identities of the abusers questionable. Also, patently false R-memories often contain important truth on a feeling level for the rememberer, which can be used if the false memory is not dealt with as if it were factual.

False and garbled R-memories no doubt comprise the majority of all R-memories of abuse today, but we must not forget that there are also true R-memories of abuse. Even our garbled R-memories contained major elements of truth. Then there are the cases that are not garbled, where the central elements of the R-memory, e.g., childhood incestuous abuse by an adult family member, are true. R-memories may be correct as to the identity of the abuser and the essential facts of the abuse.

Most of us are willing to discount all R-memories of alien abduction and satanic ritual abuse as too unlikely and "exotic" for serious consideration. Incestuous abuse we know is fairly common, however and, since some R-memories of incestuous abuse are true, it calls for the open attitude towards R-memories of incest

CONCLUSION

we have recommended on these pages.

R-memories evoked in therapy practices which devote special time and energy to unearthing them should be regarded with suspicion. The memories unearthed are suspect, as is the usefulness of the "therapy" by means of which the memories are developed. The credentials of such therapists are often excellent, and what is needed is not new or tougher laws governing the practice of therapy, but increased public awareness of the risks and hazards that regressive psychotherapy and searching for R-memories pose. New legislation is not in order.

When our first *Newsletter* article on the subject was written, few people had heard of "recovered memories." Today it is hard to pick up a newspaper without an article about a case involving them. They are a phenomenon of our time. The hysteria about childhood sexual abuse in the past decade compares with the witchcraft hysteria that swept over Europe and America in the seventeenth century. Instead of unsubstantiated charges of witchcraft against innocent women and men, today we have unsubstantiated charges of incestuous abuse of children against innocent parents. Instead of authorities unearthing visions of witches casting spells, turning into animals, and other evils, psychotherapists unearth visions of parents sexually misusing, raping, sodomizing their own children. Three centuries have not advanced us as much as we would like to believe. It is time now that these visions be laid to rest.

Glossary

amnesia: Massive forgetting, usually in consequence of a frightening or painful situation or episode in life. May have a physical cause, e.g., a brain concussion. Traumatic stress amnesia is a major repression of memories in consequence of shock or extreme stress, and is rather rare. True recovered memories (R-memories) of childhood sex abuse, as opposed to false or garbled R-memories of abuse, are normally the consequence of recovery from traumatic stress amnesia for the abuse.

assisted memory: Recovered memories that appear with the assistance of a mental health professional of some kind, perhaps through hypnosis, dream work, guided imagery etc.

confabulation: The filling in of gaps in memory by unconscious fabrication.

false memory: A pseudomemory—a memory-like mental construction of an event that did not in fact take place. Coined for and usually used to describe fictional memories of sexual abuse, satanic ritual abuse, or abduction and abuse by extraterrestrial alien beings. Often develop in a course of a therapy or a self-help program designed to recover lost memories.

False Memory Syndrome (FMS): "A condition in which a person's identity and interpersonal relationships are centered around a memory of traumatic experience which is objectively false but in which the person strongly believes."[74] The key characteristic is not the false memory itself—we all have inaccurate memories—but the orientation of one's

GLOSSARY

life around a false memory of trauma. That orientation can gravely interfere with other aspects of life—work, family, relationships, etc.

FMSF: False Memory Syndrome Foundation; founded in 1992, the FMSF defines itself as an organization which aims to seek the reasons for, prevent new cases of, and aid the victims of FMS, and to educate the public on the subject.

hysteric: In popular usage, an irrational, over-emotional woman. In Freudian parlance, a person, typically but not necessarily female, who displays strong psycho-somatic symptoms, dissociation, and/or unhealthy, extreme emotionalism, and may in therapy develop false memories of childhood incest. In Radix personal growth work, a character type that has an alive, highly charged pelvis and strong chronic tensions in eyes, throat, chest, and diaphragm. The hysteric is characterized by episodes of feeling overwhelmed by emotion, escalation of feelings, precocious and intense sexuality, problems in human relations, suggestibility, and a high creative and artistic potential.

incest: Sexual intercourse between family members, usually father/daughter, mother/son, or brother/sister but including others so closely related that marriage between them is illegal.

incestuous abuse: occurs when there is incestuous sexual contact that is not consensual, including the case where one participant is a minor and so unable to give legal consent.

Multiple Personality Disorder (MPD): A dissociative mental disorder characterized by the existence of two or more distinct personalities within one individual, each of which becomes dominant and controls behavior at times.[75] Until recently, considered extremely rare. In recent years and amid some controversy, MPD has become commonly diagnosed by some therapists, most often in the context of a supposed history of sexual or satanic ritual abuse.

perpetrator: Abuser, a person who commits acts of physical or sexual abuse. Many activist and feminist groups and some clinicians favor the term "perpetrator", although "abuser" seems to be more accurate and appropriate. Compare with ***survivor***, below.

Post-Traumatic Stress Disorder (PTSD): An anxiety disorder characterized by an origin in the horrors of military combat or other unusually distressing event (the "trauma") that causes shock, plus symptoms which may include amnesia for the trauma, numbing or reduced involvement with the external world, and often hyperalertness, sleep disturbance, survivor's guilt, and other symptoms.[76] In recent years the term has been employed extensively by therapists to victims of real and imagined incest, **satanic ritual abuse**, and **Multiple Personality Disorder**.

Radix®: A program of personal growth based on the concept of a life force in the body (the *radix*) responsible for consciousness, and a muscular armor through which a measure of control of the life force may be exercised.

recovered memories (R-memories): Memories that develop a period of time, often years or decades, after the remembered incident supposedly took place. R-memories may be recovered memories of actual events, pseudomemories, or a mixture. R-memory is the preferred term when it is possible that the "memory" is not true.

regress: (regression) To go backward in memory and/or behavior to an earlier time in one's life. Age regression is a going back that may be induced in someone by hypnosis or suggestion by another party, often a therapist. "Regressed memories" is a term loosely applied to memories of an earlier time remembered through age regression.

regressive therapy: Psychotherapy focussed on getting the client to regress to an earlier period in life, often in search of memories of trauma.

repress: (repressed; repression) To exclude material from consciousness because it is painful or unpleasant. Used for less traumatic and massive exclusion from consciousness than amnesia.

retractor (or recanter): A person who has recovered memories of abuse and eventually decided their R-memories are false, and therefore retracted stories of abuse based on their R-memories.

satanic ritual abuse (SRA): Abuse taking place in the context of a group belief in and ritual worship of an evil supernatural being or beings. It is said to include sexual abuse of all kinds, mutilation, torture, forced cannibalism, and infant sacrifice.

survivor: A term employed by some to designate a victim of incest or other sexual and physical abuse. Compare with *perpetrator*, above.

Notes

1. These figures were obtained by phone in March 1994 from the National Committee for Prevention of Child Abuse, (312) 663-3520. Further information is available in the *National Child Abuse and Neglect Data System Working Paper 2*, published by the National Center on Child Abuse and Neglect, Gaithersburg, MD. Telephone (800) FYI-3366.

2. From *The FMS Foundation Newsletter*, 2 (6), June 3, 1993, p. 6. The address of the Foundation is 3401 Market St. Suite 130, Philadelphia, PA 19104. Newsletter subscription is $20 per year.

3. In addition to *The FMS Foundation Newsletter*, see especially *True Stories of False Memories*, 1993, Eleanor Goldstein and Kevin Farmer, Boca Raton, FL: SIRS Books. To order, send $16.95 plus $2 fourth class postage to SIRS Books, P.O. Box 2348, Boca Raton, FL 33427-2348 or fax your order to (407) 994-4704.

4. See the Glossary for definitions of "retractor," "R-memory," and other new terms.

5. *The Retractor: Newsletter for Survivors of Recovered Memory Therapy*, 1992-4. Currently out of print. Retractors also have a nationwide phone and computer support network. Write M. Gavigan for information, P.O. Box 5012, Reno, NV 69513.

6. From *The FMS Foundation Newsletter*, 2 (9), October 1993, p. 1.

7. Jane Doe, "How Could This Happen? Coping with a False Accusation of Incest and Rape" in *Issues in Child Abuse Accusations*, 3 (3), pp.154-65. Published anonymously, the article was later attributed to Pamela Freyd.

8. Jennifer Freyd, *Theoretical and Personal Perspectives on the Delayed Memory Debate*. Obtained from the author, care of the Psychology Department, University of Oregon, Eugene, OR 97403. A presentation given August 7, 1993 to the Center for Mental Health at Foote Hospital's Continuing Education Conference in Ann Arbor, MI.

9. Ellen Bass and Laura Davis, 1988, *The Courage to Heal: A Guide for Women Survivors of Child Sexual Abuse*. New York: HarperCollins Publishers. This is the primary manual for therapists endeavoring to unearth R-memories of sexual abuse in their clients.

10. A summary of the positions of each appeared as "Memories of a Disputed Past" by Jann Mitchell in Oregon's largest daily paper, *The Oregonian*, August 8, 1993.

11. From Mark F. Schwartz, Sc.D., "False Memory Blues: An Editorial" in *Masters and Johnson Report* 2 (1), Summer 1993, p. 3.

12. See, for example, "Traumatic Therapy," *True Stories of False Memories*, p. 373.

13. Ian M. L. Hunter, 1969, *Memory*. London: Pelican Books, p. 86. This is an excellent non-technical book on memory. See also: Elizabeth Loftus, *Memory*. Reading, MA: Addison-Wesley, 1980.

14. R. S. Woodworth reviews some of the classical experiments in this area, including his own, in *Experimental Psychology*, New York, Henry Holt and Co., 1938.

15. See, for example, Sigmund Freud, 1951, *The Psychopathology of Everyday Life*. New York: Mentor Books. The original German work dates to the beginning of this century.

16. See especially the paper by Elizabeth Loftus, 1993, "The Reality of Repressed Memories." *American Psychologist*, 48 (5), May.

17. See the Glossary for definition of the term "hysteric." Some characteristics of the hysteric character structure are discussed in Chapter Five.

18. From Sigmund Freud, 1938, *The Basic Writings of Sigmund Freud*. New York: The Modern Library, p. 940. Original publication in English dates to 1910.

19. See Jeffrey Masson, 1985: *The Assault on Truth: Freud's Suppression of the Seduction Theory*. New York: Penguin Books. Many articles in the popular press at the time referred to this work.

20. The story of the implanted "memory" of being lost in a shopping mall is described by psychologist Elizabeth Loftus in "The Reality of Repressed Memories." *American Psychologist*, 48 (5), May 1993.

21. The story appeared in *The FMS Foundation Newsletter*, 2 (5), May 3 1993, p. 5.

22. From Paul McHugh, 1992, "Psychiatric Misadventures," in *American Scholar*, Autumn, 61, pp. 507-508.

23. From John F. Kihlstrom, 1993, *The Recovery of Memory in the Laboratory and Clinic*. Obtained from the author. A presentation given to the 1993 joint convention of the Rocky Mountain Psychological Association and the Western Psychological Association.

24. To fully understand retractor stories, read them in toto. The best collection known to us is Eleanor Goldstein and Kevin Farmer's *True Stories of False Memories*, available from SIRS Books (see Note 3).

25. From Renee Fredrickson, 1992, *Repressed Memories: A Journey to Recovery from Sexual Abuse*. New York: Simon and Schuster, p. 32.

26. From "Diagnosed as MPD" in *True Stories of False Memories*, pp. 393-4. This and all other quotations from the book with permission from SIRS Books.

27. From "Surviving 'Therapy'," *True Stories of False Memories*, pp. 319-20.

28. Ellen Bass and Laura Davis, 1988, *The Courage to Heal: A Guide for Women Survivors of Child Sexual Abuse*.

29. From "Traumatic Therapy," *True Stories of False Memories*, p. 377.

30. From Melody Gavigan in *The Retractor: Newsletter for Survivors of Recovered Memory Therapy*, December 1992, p.3.

31. Quoted in Elizabeth Loftus, 1993, "Repressed Memories of Childhood Trauma: Are They Genuine?" *The Harvard Mental Health Newsletter*, 9 (8), February.

32. From "The Truth Set Me Free," *True Stories of False Memories*, p. 334.

33. From *The FMS Foundation Newsletter*, 2 (11), December 1993, p. 8.

34. From "My Recovery from 'Recovery'," *True Stories of False Memories*, pp. 253-4.

35. From "Surviving 'Therapy'," *True Stories of False Memories*, p. 306.

36. From "Jennifer's Story," *The Retractor: Newsletter for Survivors of Recovered Memory Therapy*, Summer 1993, p. 4.

37. From "Memories Not Mine," *True Stories of False Memories*, p. 223-4.

38. From "Misplaced Trust," *True Stories of False Memories*, p. 355.

39. A retractor quoted by Melody Gavigan in *The Retractor: Newsletter for Survivors of Recovered Memory Therapy*, Summer 1993, p. 1.

40. From Melody Gavigan in *The Retractor: Newsletter for Survivors of Recovered Memory Therapy*, Summer 1993, p. 1.

41. From "Surviving 'Therapy'," *True Stories of False Memories*, pp. 315-6.

42. From "Diagnosed as MPD," *True Stories of False Memories*, p. 390.

43. From Surviving "Therapy'," *True Stories of False Memories*, pp. 327-8.

44. From "Misplaced Trust," *True Stories of False Memories*, p. 364.

45. From "Surviving 'Therapy'," *True Stories of False Memories*, p. 314.

46. From "Traumatic Therapy," *True Stories of False Memories*, p. 382-3.

47. From "Lucy's Story," *The Retractor: Newsletter for Survivors of Recovered Memory Therapy*, Winter 1993, p. 7.

48. Glenn Kessler, in an article in Long Island *Newsday*, quoted in the December 1993 issue of *The FMS Foundation Newsletter*, 2 (11), p. 4.

49. Quoted in *The FMS Foundation Newsletter*, 2 (11), December 1993, p. 4.

50. From Paul McHugh, 1992, "Psychiatric Misadventures," *American Scholar*, 61, Autumn.

51. Radix teaching is a personal growth profession with three hundred practitioners worldwide. It was created by Charles and Erica Kelley twenty-five years ago. The case of Martha (p. 63) illustrates the work.

Not all Radix teachers handle regression as recommended in these pages. K/R Publications offers information about the method.

52. For examples, see Martin Gardner, "Notes of a Fringe Watcher: The False Memory Syndrome," *Skeptical Inquirer*, 17, Summer 1993, 370-375; and Paul Gray, "The Assault on Freud," *Time*, 142, Nov. 29, 1993, pp. 46-49+.

53. Michelle Smith and L. Pazder, 1981, *Michelle Remembers*. New York: Pocket Books.

54. *Satanic Ritual Abuse: The Current State of Knowledge*. Special issue of *The Journal of Psychology and Theology*, 20 (3), Fall 1992. To order, send $9 to the *Journal* at Rosemead School of Psychology, Biola University, 13800 Biola Ave., La Mirada, CA 90639.

55. B. Bottoms, P. Shaver, and G. Goodman, 1991, *Profile of Ritualistic and Religion-Related Abuse Allegations Reported to Clinical Psychologists in the United States*. Presented at the 99th Annual Convention of the American Psychological Association, San Francisco.

56. Ruth E. Shaffer, and Louis J. Cozolino, 1992, "Adults Who Report Childhood Ritualistic Abuse," *The Journal of Psychology and Theology*, 20 (3), Fall, 188-193.

57. See also David M. Jacobs, 1992, *Secret Life: Firsthand Documented Accounts of UFO Abductions*, New York: Simon and Schuster; and John Mack, 1994, *Abductions*, New York: Scribner.

58. Wheeler, et al., 1993, "An Experimental Assessment of Facilitated Communication," *Mental Retardation*, 31 (1), February, pp. 49-60.

59. See Wilhelm Reich, 1948, *The Function of the Orgasm*, and 1949, *Character Analysis*, third edition. New York: Orgone Institute Press. Reissued by Farrar, Strauss and Gireaux. My own approach to the armor is discussed briefly in the monographs, Kelley, 1988, *Body Contact in Radix Work*, and in depth in the compilation of my work, 1993b, *Radix Personal Growth Work*, Vancouver, WA: K/R Publications.

60. From C. R. Kelley, 1974, *Education in Feeling and Purpose*, second edition. Vancouver, WA: K/R Publications, p. 41. Included in 1993b, a compilation.

61. Perls' technique for dreamwork involved acting out the characters and the objects in a dream, with facilitator guidance.

62. See A. Kroker, and M. Kroker, Eds., 1991, *The Hysterical Male: Essays in New Feminist Theory*. New York: St. Martins Press.

63. For a description of Dr. Barbara Koopman's penlight technique in Reichian work, see Baker, Elsworth, 1967, *Man in the Trap*, pp. 50-52, New York: The Macmillan Co.

64. From "Surviving 'Therapy'," *True Stories of False Memories*, p. 309-10.

65. Ellen Bass and Laura Davis, 1988, *The Courage to Heal: A Guide for Women Survivors of Child Sexual Abuse*.

66. From "Traumatic Therapy," *True Stories of False Memories*, p. 374.

67. From *The FMS Foundation Newsletter*, 2 (9), October 1993, p. 9.

68. From *The FMS Foundation Newsletter*, 2 (9), October 1993, p. 10.

69. From Mark Smith, 1993, "Haunted Dreams: Real or Implanted?" *The Houston Chronicle*, September 12.

70. Left on the answering machine of the FMS Foundation. Quoted in *The FMS Foundation Newsletter*, 2 (7), July 3, 1993, p. 9.

71. Write to *The Chuck Kelley Newsletter*, 13717 SE 36th St., Steamboat Landing, Vancouver, WA 98684. Unless writer specifies otherwise, letters may be published in whole or part, with the writer's name.

72. See especially Thomas Szasz, 1984, *The Therapeutic State*. Buffalo, NY: Prometheus Books; and 1961, *The Myth of Mental Illness: Foundations of a Theory of Personal Conduct*. New York: Hoeber-Harper.

73. See especially Reuven Bar-Levav, 1988, *Thinking in the Shadow of Feelings*. New York: Simon and Schuster.

74. Dr. John F. Kihlstrom, quoted in literature from the False Memory Syndrome Foundation, September 1993.

75. Summarized from the *Diagnostic and Statistical Manual of Mental Disorders* (third edition). American Psychiatric Association. Washington, D.C.: APA, 1980, pp. 257-259.

76. From the *Diagnostic and Statistical Manual of Mental Disorders* (third edition), pp. 236-238.

References

American Psychiatric Association, 1980, *Diagnostic and Statistical Manual of Mental Disorders* (third edition). Washington, DC: APA.

Baker, Elsworth, 1967, *Man in the Trap*. New York: The Macmillan Co.

Bar-Levav, Reuven, 1988, *Thinking in the Shadow of Feelings*. New York: Simon and Schuster.

Bass, Ellen, & Davis, Laura, 1988, *The Courage to Heal: A Guide for Women Survivors of Child Sexual Abuse*. New York: HarperCollins.

Bottoms, B., Shaver, P., and Goodman, G., 1991, "Profile of Ritualistic and Religion-Related Abuse Allegations Reported to Clinical Psychologists in the United States." Presented at the 99th Annual Convention of the American Psychological Association, San Francisco.

Doe, Jane, 1991. See Freyd, Pamela.

The False Memory Syndrome Foundation Newsletter. Published eleven times annually. Philadelphia: FMS Foundation.

Fredrickson, Renee, 1992, *Repressed Memories: A Journey to Recovery from Sexual Abuse*. New York: Simon and Schuster.

Freud, Sigmund, 1951, *The Psychopathology of Everyday Life*. New York: Mentor Books. Original publication date unknown.

_____, 1938, *The Basic Writings of Sigmund Freud*. New York: The Modern Library. Original publications of this compilation date to the early years of this century.

Freyd, Jennifer, 1993, "Theoretical and Personal Perspectives on the Delayed Memory Debate." Obtained from the author. A presentation given August 7, 1993 to the Center for Mental Health at Foote Hospital's Continuing Education Conference in Ann Arbor, MI.

Freyd, Pamela (Published as Doe, Jane), 1991, "How Could This Happen? Coping with a False Accusation of Incest and Rape," *Issues in Child Abuse Accusations*, 3 (3), 154-65.

Gardner, Martin, 1993, "Notes of a Fringe Watcher: The False Memory Syndrome," *Skeptical Inquirer*, 17, Summer, 370-375.

Goldstein, Eleanor, and Farmer, Kevin, 1993, *True Stories of False Memories*. Boca Raton, FL: SIRS Books.

Hunter, Ian M. L., 1969, *Memory: Facts and Fallacies*. London: Pelican Books.

Jacobs, David M., 1992, *Secret Life: Firsthand Documented Accounts of UFO Abductions*. New York: Simon and Schuster.

Kelley, Charles R., 1993a, "Recovery of Repressed Memories," Parts I, II, III. *The Chuck Kelley Radix Newsletter* 13, 14, 15, Winter, Spring, Fall. Vancouver, WA: K/R Publications.

_____, 1993b, *The Radix, Volume I: Radix Personal Growth Work*. Vancouver, WA: K/R Publications. A compilation.

_____, 1988, *Body Contact in Radix Work*. Vancouver, WA: K/R Publications.

_____, 1974, *Education in Feeling and Purpose* (second edition). Vancouver, WA: K/R Publications. (First published by the Interscience Research Institute, 1970.)

_____, 1972, "Post-Primal and Genital Character: A Critique of Janov and Reich," *Journal of Humanistic Psychology*, 12 (2), Fall.

Kihlstrom, John F., 1993, *The Recovery of Memory in the Laboratory and Clinic*. Obtained from the author. A presentation given to the 1993 joint convention of the Rocky Mountain Psychological Association and the Western Psychological Association.

Kroker, A. and Kroker, M. Eds., 1991, *The Hysterical Male: Essays in New Feminist Theory*. New York: St. Martins Press.

Loftus, Elizabeth, 1993, "Repressed Memories of Childhood Trauma: Are They Genuine?" *The Harvard Mental Health Letter*, 9 (8), February.

———, 1993, "The Reality of Repressed Memories," *American Psychologist*, 48 (5), May.

———, 1980, *Memory*. Reading, MA: Addison-Wesley.

Mack, John, 1994, *Abductions*. New York: Scribner.

Masson, Jeffrey, 1985, *The Assault on Truth: Freud's Suppression of the Seduction Theory*. New York: Penguin Books.

McHugh, Paul, 1992, "Psychiatric Misadventures," *American Scholar*, 61, Autumn, 497-510.

Mitchell, Jann, 1993, "Memories of a Disputed Past," *The Oregonian*, August 8.

Reich, Wilhelm, 1949, *Character Analysis* (third edition). New York: Orgone Institute Press. Reissued by Farrar, Strauss and Gireaux.

———, 1948, *The Function of the Orgasm*. New York: Orgone Institute Press. Reissued by Farrar, Strauss and Gireaux.

The Retractor: Newsletter for Survivors of Recovered Memory Therapy. (Melody Gavigan, Ed.) Published quarterly. Reno, NV.

Rogers, Martha, 1992, "A Call for Discernment—Natural and Spiritual," *The Journal of Psychology and Theology*, 20 (3), Fall, 175-186.

Schwartz, Mark F. 1993, "False Memory Blues: An Editorial," *Masters and Johnson Report* 2 (1), Summer, 3.

Shaffer, Ruth E. and Cozolino, Louis J., 1992, "Adults Who Report Childhood Ritualistic Abuse," *The Journal of Psychology and Theology*, 20 (3), Fall, 188-193.

Smith, Mark, 1993, "Haunted Dreams: Real or Implanted?" *The Houston Chronicle*, September 12, 1993.

Smith, Michelle, and Pazder, L., 1981, *Michelle Remembers*. New York: Pocket Books.

Szasz, Thomas, 1984, *The Therapeutic State*. Buffalo, NY: Prometheus Books.

_____, 1961, *The Myth of Mental Illness: Foundations of a Theory of Personal Conduct*. New York: Hoeber-Harper.

Wheeler, Douglas L., Jacobson, John W., Paglieri, Raymond A. and Schwartz, Allen A., 1993, "An Experimental Assessment of Facilitated Communication," *Mental Retardation*, 31 (1), February, 49-60.

Woodworth, Roger S., 1938, *Experimental Psychology*. New York, Henry Holt and Co.

Index

Abney, Lucy, 39, 83-84

Abuse, childhood sexual. *See also* Abuse cases; Incest; Memories of abuse; Rape; Satanic ritual abuse; Symptoms; Victim
dealing with, <u>59-68</u>, 69-78
effects of, 62
reporting of, ix-xi, 3, 43
prevalence of, 3, 5, 60

Abuse cases, 5-7, 61-62. *See also* Accusations; R-memory cases; Retractor cases
Jan, 49
Martha, 6, 43, <u>63-64</u>, 65-66, 103
Shirley, <u>4-5</u>, 103

Abuser, xi, 12, 109. *See also* Perpetrator
action against, ix, 79-80, 81
misidentification of, 19-23

Accusations (of abuse), xi, 22 23, 57-58
examples of, 7, 11-12
false, xi, 4, 7, 8-9, 13, 22, 28-30
retracted, xi, 9
based on R-memories, x, xi, 8, 9, 11, 22, 28-30, 53, 83

Alien abduction, x, 45, <u>51-52</u>, 53, 56, 88, 91, 95, 105, 108

Amnesia, xi, 16, 19, 86, 87, <u>108</u>, 110

Anger, 62, 66, 74, 75, 76, <u>80-81</u>

Anti-therapeutic, 68, 79, 87

Armor. *See* Muscular armor

Arnold, Roseanne Barr, xi

Autism, 55-56
normal autism, 95

Backlash. *See also*: Denial, FMS claims as
against therapists, 43
false memory claims as, 8

Baker, Ellen, 99-104

Bar-Levav, Reuven, 92, 94-97

Bass, Ellen, 91. *See also Courage to Heal, The*

Belief systems, 42
and R-memories, <u>52-55</u>

Bernardin, Cardinal, xi, xii

Bodywork, <u>60</u>, 63-64, 69, 74, 93-94, 98, 99-100, 110

Body memories, 31

Bottoms et al., 47
Brothers. *See also* Siblings
  abuse by, 5
  accusations against, 21, 28
Celebrities, xi
Chuck Kelley's Radix Newsletter, xii, 85, note 71, 87, 107
Cierpial, Ralphine, 97-98
Commentary by readers, 85-104
  Ellen Baker, 99-104
  Reuven Bar-Levav, 94-96
  Ralphine Cierpial, 97-98
  European therapist, 85-88
  Alice Ladas, 93-94
  Judith Searle, 89-93
  Roger Wescott, 88-89
Confabulation, 15, 85-86, 108
Confrontation (of alleged abuser), 62, 80
Conversion Disorder, 92
Courage To Heal, The, 12 (note 9), 23, 36, 79-80
Cozolino, Louis and Shaffer, Ruth, 47-49
Cults
  religious, 93
  R-memory therapy as, 42, 50
  satanic, 48, 50, 83. *See also* Satanic ritual abuse
Davis, Laura, 36, 91. *See also Courage to Heal, The*
Daycare cases, 57
Denial (of abuse), ix, 29, 48
  FMS claims as, 8, 10, 12-13
  "in denial", 21, 28, 32, 35, 36, 37, 79
Diagnostic and Statistical Manual of Mental Disorders [DSM III], 109-110 (notes 75, 76)

Disclosure of abuse, ix, 48
Dissociation, 47, 48, 69, 86, 98
  and hysteria, 71, 72, 74, 77, 109
Dissociative disorders, 82, 109
Doe, Jane. *See* Freyd, Pamela
Dreams, 26, 29, 88. *See also* Nightmares
Dream work, 27-28, 71, 102, 108
Drugs
  addiction to, 39
  use of in therapy, 39, 77
Emotions, 42-43
Eyes. *See* Ocular segment
Facilitated communication (FC), 55-56
False memories. *See* Memories, false
False Memory Syndrome (FMS), 108
False Memory Syndrome Foundation (FMSF), xiii, note 2, 8-9, 10, 11-12, 109. *See also FMS Foundation Newsletter*
  critics of, 10, 12, 13
Fathers, 70-71, 101, 103
  abuse by, 61-2
  accusations against, xi, 7, 12-13, 22, 32, 34, 49, 83
Family, 12, 37, 38, 82, 99, 103
  of choice, 35, 38
Fantasy, x, 65, 70, 71, 77, 84, 102, 104, 105
FBI, 50
Feminists, 18, 41, 53, 77, 103, 109
FMS Foundation Newsletter, 7 (note 2), 9, 10, 32 (note 33), 40 (notes 48, 49), 83 (notes 67, 68), 84 (note 70)
Fredrickson, Renee, 25, 91

INDEX

Freud, Sigmund, 15-16, 16-18, 71, 74, 88, 89, 92, 97, 105

Freyd, Jennifer, 11-12

Freyd, Pamela, xiii, 11 (note 7), 12

Freyd, Peter, 11, 12

Frontline, 56

Fugue state, 16

Gavigan, Melody. *See Retractor, The: Newsletter for Survivors of Recovered Memory Therapy*; Retractor cases, "My Recovery from 'Recovery'"

Gondolf, Lynn. *See* Retractor cases, "Traumatic Therapy"

Grandfather
  abuse by, 4-5
  accusations against, 19-20, 22, 49, 83

Groups. *See* Group therapy; Support groups; Twelve-step programs

Group therapy, 33, 35, 60, 77, 78-79, 81-82

Hospitalization (psychiatric), 11, 31, 32-33, 39, 48

Hunter, Ian, 14

Hypnosis, x, 16, 108, 110. *See also* Self-hypnosis

Hysteric character, 17, 17-18, 71, 72-74, 92-93, 101, 103-104, 109
  and R-memories, 16, 50, 74
  working with, 74-78, 103

Identification of abusers, errors in, 19-23, 29

Incest, 109. *See also* Memories; R-memories
  types of, 5-7
  "survivors'" groups, 60, 78-79, 81, 84

Incest Survivors Anonymous. *See* Twelve-step programs

Insurance (payment for therapy), 39, 40, 53, 54, 90

Intermediaries. *See also* Belief systems
  and autism, 55-56
  in R-memories, 54, 55, 57, 58,

Jacobs, David, note 57

Jan (SRA case study), 49

Journal of Psychology and Theology, 46, note 54

Kihlstrom, John, 23-24, 108 (note 74)

Koopman, Barbara, note 63

Ladas, Alice, 93-94

Laurel case, 20-21, 22, 28-30, 106

Lawsuits, xi, 9, 10, 39, 79

Little Rascals daycare case, 57

Loftus, Elizabeth, 18-19, 32 (note 31)

Los Angeles Times (phone survey), 3

Mack, John, note 57

Martha case, 6, 43, 63-64, 65-66, 103

Masson, Jeffrey, 17-18

McHugh, Paul, 22, 40-41

McMartin preschool case, 57

Memories, of abuse
  assisted, 108
  continuous, x, 4, 33, 60-68
  dealing with, 59-84. *See also* R-memories, dealing with
  disbelief of, ix, 87
  dredging for, 23-42
  effects on the body of, 62
  false, xi, 8, 108
  interpreting, 30, 52, 71

muscular armor and, 62
pseudomemories. *See* Memories, false
psychotherapy for, 59-60
Radix work with; Martha's case, 63-66
regression and, 66-68
self-help for, 60

Memory
amnesia, 15
confabulation and "filling in," 15
fugue and, 15-16
nature of, 14-24
recovery of. *See* R-memories
right and wrong of, 22
suggestion and, 18
uncertainty of, 14

Michelle Remembers, <u>46</u>, 87

Mother
abuse by, 6, 93
accusations against, 83, 84

Multiple Personality Disorder (MPD), 32, 40-41, 53, <u>109</u>

Muscular armor, <u>43</u>, <u>62</u>, note 59, 64-65, 66, 67, 81, 103, 110. *See also* Reich, Wilhelm

Mythical truth (in R-memories), 70-71

National Committee for the Investigation of Aerial Phenomena (NICAP), 52

National Committee for the Prevention of Child Abuse (NCPCA), x

Newsday, 40

Nightmares, 21, 26, 35. *See also* Dreams

Ocular segment, 66, 67, 98

Pasley, Laura. *See* Retractor cases, "Misplaced Trust"

Past lives, x, 45, 46, 71

Patriarchy, 99, 103

Perls, Fritz, 71, note 61

Perpetrator, 12, 13, 37, 41, 48, 53, 82, <u>109</u>. *See also* Abuser

Personal growth, 92, 97. *See also* Radix

Postmodernist, 73-74

Post-Traumatic Stress Disorder (PTSD), 53, <u>109</u>

Primal therapy, 67-68

Pseudomemories. *See* Memories, false

Psychotherapy, psychotherapists. *See* Therapy

R-memories
accuracy of, 9
of alien abduction, 51-52
bad therapy and, 79-82
and belief systems, 52-55
commentary concerning, 85-104
conclusions concerning, 105-107
dealing with, 68-78
definition, x-xii, <u>110</u>
doubts about, <u>35-36</u>, 37, 68, 78-79, 83, 84
errors of (identifying abusers), 19-23, 20, 29
examples of, 19-20, 20-22, 22
of fantastic events, 45-46
Freud and, 16-17
group development of false, 78-79
how *not* to deal with, 78
hysteria and, 71-74
implanting of, 18-19
intermediaries in recovering, 53-58
manufacture of, 25-27, 27-28,
meaning of false, 70-71
and MPD, 40-42, 54

INDEX

myth in dealing with, 71
principles and suggestions for dealing with, 74-78
professional help with, 69
pseudo-reality based on false, 82-84
psychiatric diagnoses and, 92
and psychotherapy, 25-44
retraction of, 26-39
of satanic ritual abuse (SRA), 46-51
suggestibility and, 72-73
and symptoms of incest, 30-31, 32
and therapy fees, 11
true, false, or garbled, xi-xii
victim attitude and false, 84

R-memory cases, 83, 83-84, 100-101. *See also* Accusations; Retractor cases
Laurel case, 20-21, 28-30.

Radix, 41, note 51, 67-68, 90, 92, 110

Ramona, Gary, xi

Rape, 5, 6, 7, 93

Regress, 110

Regression, 65, 75, 77, 99-100, 102, 108

Regressive techniques, x, 28, 47, 66-67, 79, 99-100

Regressive therapy, x, 17, 46, 67-68, 82, 110

Reich, Wilhelm, 43, 62, 88, 90, 92

Repression, 15-16, 19, 26, 99, 110. *See also* Memories

Retractor, xiii, 9-10, 24, 84, 105, 110

Retractor cases, 10, 84;
"Diagnosed with MPD," 26-27 (note 26), 37 (note 42)
"Jennifer's Story," 33-34 (note 36)
Lucy Abney, 39, 83-84
"Memories Not Mine," 34 (note 37)
"Misplaced Trust," 35 (note 38), 38 (note 44)
"My Recovery from '"Recovery',"
33 (note 34)
"Surviving 'Therapy'," 27-28 (note 27), 33 (note 35), 36 (note 41), 37 (note 43), 38 (note 45), 78-79 (note 64)
"The Truth Set Me Free," 32 (note 32)
"Traumatic Therapy," 31 (note 29), 39 (note 46), 81-82 (note 66)

Retractor, The: Newsletter for Survivors of Recovered Memory Therapy, 9 (note 5), 31 (note 30), 36 (notes 39, 40), 39

Revenge, 79-81

Ritual, 88-89. *See also* Satanic ritual abuse

Rubin, Jay, 20-22, 28-30, 106

Satanic ritual abuse (SRA), 26-27, 46-51, note 54, 52, 54, 83-84, 88, 96, 110

Schwartz, Mark, 12

Searle, Judith, 89-93

Seduction theory, 17-18

Self-hypnosis, 27, 28, 35. *See also* Hypnosis

Shaffer, Ruth and Cozolino, Louis, 47-49

Shirley, 4-5, 103

Siblings, 9, 38. *See also* Brother; Sister

Sister, 10, 83. *See also* Siblings

Smith, Mark, 83-84

Social hysteria, 91, 107

Social pressure, 35

Sodomy, 5

Stepfather
  abuse by, 63
  suggestibility, 18
  of children, 57
  of hysterics, 71-73

Suggestion, by therapist, <u>18-19</u>, 25, 32-33, 46

Suicide, 48, 81-82, 84

Suing, xi, 79. *See also* Lawsuits

Support groups, 38. *See also* Group therapy

Survivor, 110

Symptoms
  interpretation of, 2, <u>30</u>, <u>31</u>, 33
  of abuse, 59-60, 62, 86

Szasz, Thomas, 91

Tavris, Carol, 91

Television, 91, 92

Tellington Jones, Linda, 93

Therapy, 41, 90-93, 94, 96, 107. *See also* Bodywork; Cults; Regressive therapy
  vs. personal growth, 92, 97

Trauma, 42-43

Traumatic amnesia. *See* Amnesia

True Stories of False Memories, xiii, note 3

Twelve-step programs, 48, 60

UFOs, 52. *See also* Alien abduction

Uncle
  accusations against, 22, 49
  abuse by, 20, 33

Victim, 86, 88, 94-95, 98, <u>110</u>
  two classes of, 4

Victim character attitude, 39, 79, 91, 94-95

Wescott, Roger, 88-89

Wheeler et al., 56 (note 58)

Witch hunt, 40-41, 52, 54, 58

Witnesses, in court, 14

Woodworth, Robert, note 14

Zealots and R-memories. *See* Belief systems